JUSTIN R. ELLIS

REPRESENTATION, RESISTANCE AND THE DIGIQUEER

Fighting for Recognition in Technocratic Times

BRISTOL
UNIVERSITY
PRESS

First published in Great Britain in 2023 by

Bristol University Press
University of Bristol
1–9 Old Park Hill
Bristol
BS2 8BB
UK
t: +44 (0)117 374 6645
e: bup-info@bristol.ac.uk

Details of international sales and distribution partners are available at
bristoluniversitypress.co.uk

British Library Cataloguing in Publication Data
A catalogue record for this book is available from the British Library

ISBN 978-1-5292-2871-7 hardcover
ISBN 978-1-5292-2872-4 ePub
ISBN 978-1-5292-2873-1 ePdf

Cover design: Bristol University Press
Front cover image: shutterstock/kentoh
Bristol University Press use environmentally responsible
print partners.
Printed in Great Britain by CPI Group (UK) Ltd, Croydon, CR0 4YY

To my mother Robyn Elizabeth Ellis

Contents

About the Author

Dr Justin Ellis' research examines the relationship between digital media technologies, institutional trust and politically vulnerable populations, in particular LGBTQ+ communities. His scholarship on these issues is regularly published in high-ranking internationally peer-reviewed journals. Justin's 2021 monograph *Policing Legitimacy: Social Media, Scandal and Sexual Citizenship* critically analyses the relationship between LGBTQ+ identity-based rights claims, police accountability, and the regulation of digital platforms. Justin is Senior Lecturer in Criminology at the University of Newcastle School of Law and Justice and Editor-in-Chief of *Current Issues in Criminal Justice*, the journal of the Institute of Criminology at the Sydney Law School.

Acknowledgements

Thank you to Emerita Professor Gail Mason, Dr Marianne Colbran, and my partner Mr Nacanieli Cagilaba for reviewing a draft of the manuscript, and to Professor Thomas Crofts, who read a chapter of the manuscript. Thank you to my colleagues at the University of Newcastle School of Law and Justice and at the Institute of Criminology at the Sydney Law School for their time and investment in critical debate on many of the issues discussed in this book. Rebecca Tomlinson, criminology editor, and Becky Taylor, law editor, and the team at Bristol University Press provided great support throughout. Thank you to the reviewers of the proposal and the reviewers of the manuscript, and to Mr Andy Quan, who provided editorial guidance in the final stages of preparing the manuscript. Any errors are my own.

Some of the themes in this book have been drawn from the following publications and are reproduced with permission:

Ellis, J.R. (2022a) 'A fairy tale gone wrong: social media, recursive hate and the politicisation of Drag Queen Storytime', *The Journal of Criminal Law*, 86(2): 94–108.

Ellis, J.R. (2022b) 'Blurred consent and redistributed privacy: owning LGBTQ identity in surveillance capitalism', in D.M.D. Silva and M. Deflem (eds) *Diversity in Criminology and Criminal Justice Studies*, Volume 27, Bingley: Emerald, pp 183–96.

growing number of bans on the use of TikTok on government devices across jurisdictions, and a broader call to limit the use of all apps over privacy concerns, further speaks to the complexities of these issues.

The spectrum of malign influence from foreign actors in the EU against LGBTQ+ people from disinformation is indicative of the breadth of representational harms against LGBTQ+ expression; false information intentionally designed to be false and misleading, and with a political, social or economic goal, that includes threats to child safety, negative othering, opposing a 'gender ideology', heteroactivism, the protection of the 'natural family's' rights, and restoring the 'natural' order as ordained by God (Strand and Svensson 2021).

This latest chapter in the contest over LGBTQ+ individual and group agency is occurring in an increasingly networked, atomized, globalized and sectarian world, despite an increase in protectionism. The uneven factual accuracy of the OpenAI chatbot, ChatGPT, looks set to further complicate the ambiguities arising from this confluence of ideology, technology and identity formation. Conservative religious organizations, domestic extremists, politicians, and right-wing and authoritarian governments, continue to invoke discredited legacies of legal, medical, and religious stigma to marginalize diverse LGBTQ+ individual and group identity. In turn, these legacies can influence how LGBTQ+ peoples are filtered and framed through social and other media representation. At the same time, digital platforms and traditional news media companies can profit from the amplification of online and in-person bias-motivated conduct (Greer and McLaughlin 2017, Ellis 2021).

The transformation of cultural production through digital media platforms has restructured the terms by which culture is distributed and paid for (Caplan and Gillespie 2020). This transformation has clarified the workings of stigma-derived anti-LGBTQ+ economic and political purchase through the hybrid media ecosystem. Twitter and Facebook comprehensively failed to enforce community standards amid a surge in hateful online anti-LGBTQ+ rhetoric triggered by Florida's 'Don't Say Gay or Trans' Bill (Center for Countering Digital Hate 2022a). Meta (Facebook) has profited from advertisements promoting hateful child 'grooming' rhetoric against the LGBTQ+ community and its allies, with at least 59 advertisements identified as promoting that rhetoric, served to users over 2.1 million times (Center for Digital Hate 2022a). The Center for Digital Hate estimates that anti-LGBTQ+ extremists are picking up followers at quadruple the pace under Elon Musk at Twitter, and that anti-LGBTQ+ 'grooming' rhetoric went viral on Twitter after the Colorado Springs shooting (Center for Countering Digital Hate 2022b).

The book argues that the manufacture of an imagined LGBTQ+ enemy, and the rationalization, normalization, and monetization of stigma based on that fiction, is amplifying representational harms through this information warfare. Examples from case law, parliamentary debates, social media, traditional news media, and LGBTQ+-tech advocacy, articulate the durable harm of stigma against LGBTQ+ expression, relations, and conduct, and the uneven fortunes of LGBTQ+ individuals and communities across the globe. The book takes an interdisciplinary approach through integration of the usually disparate themes of media representation, LGBTQ+ human rights, identity, capitalism, consumerism, and advocacy. In doing so, the book examines the role of knowledge production processes in attributing value to identity through representation (Foucault 1981, Hall 1997), and the potential of the 'digiqueer' citizen in the fight for recognition in technocratic times.

Digiqueer criminology

My first book on the 'digiqueer' focused on the power of bystander scrutiny of police excessive force through social media video (Ellis 2021). That research showed that unexpected scrutiny can pressure the police to account, and

Instagram (@gaysagainstgroomers) and YouTube accounts (Gingerich 2022), the 'outing' of teachers on TikTok, and the doxing of drag queens on far-right conspiracy news websites such as Infowars – publishing their identifying information online with malicious intent and without consent – are just some of the known consequences of representational harms derived from the stigma of same-sex attraction and related gender expression.

The monetization of bias through YouTube sites includes the sale of mundane items such as sweatshirts and mugs adorned with bias-driven, homophobic slurs, and as noted in the case of vilification of gay journalist Carlos Maza by far-right YouTuber Steven Crowder (Nett 2019). Crowder is part of an assortment of scholars, media pundits and internet celebrities that Lewis has termed the Alternative Influence Network (AIN). The AIN radicalizes through social networking practices that promote a range of political positions on YouTube, from mainstream versions of libertarianism and conservatism, all the way to overt White nationalism (Lewis 2018), and includes presenters such as Tim Pool, Joe Rogan and Jordan Peterson.

Moderation guidelines from TikTok for jurisdictions where same-sex conduct is unlawful, have resulted in the underrepresentation of diverse LGBTQ+ expression through banning any content that could be seen as positive to gay people or gay rights, down to same-sex couples holding hands, even in countries where that conduct is lawful (Hern 2019, Ryan et al 2020). At the same time, many right-wing extremists today 'no longer subscribe to the narrow concept of nationalism, but instead imagine themselves as participants in a global struggle against a global enemy' (Combating Terrorism Center at West Point 2021, p i). This shift complicates the vulnerability of LGBTQ+ people who may not be able to rely on the enforcement of the protections afforded to them based on national identity.

The platforms on which this battle over identity is playing out, are underscored by the undermining of the Western liberal democratic rights-based approach to the protection of vulnerable populations through 'technocracy'; a form of symbiotic, neoliberal governance between big tech and governments that favours policies that promote free-market capitalism and deregulation, and that has conflated commercial imperatives with technological necessity (Zuboff 2019). This symbiosis has eroded standards of privacy and consent, and transparency over decision making (Zuboff 2019, Esmark 2020). This includes 'hyper-collection': the accumulation, sorting and analysis of data by large companies in covert or passive ways beyond what a company needs, and that is not supported by a legitimate commercial or legal purpose (Walker-Munro 2022).

Shifting norms on consent have 'blurred' through data accrual on sexual identity and government aggregation of social media data with other available databases (Shephard 2016). The inequitable algorithmic sorting of populations into measurable types for security and profit through surveillance technologies can conceal hidden commercial practices of extraction, prediction and targeting (Zuboff 2019, p vi). Identity formation has thus been subordinated to a new global architecture of behaviour modification through the constant accrual of data on individuals through consumption and everyday life (Jansson 2015, Zuboff 2019).

Algorithmically filtered, discriminatory depictions can reinforce the subordination of a group based on identity, including stereotyping, recognition, denigration and underrepresentation (Mehrabi et al 2021). These depictions can include censorship of LGBTQ+, people of colour, and people with disabilities through 'shadowbanning', which blocks a user from a social media site or online forum without their knowledge (Salty 2019, Rauchberg 2022), and algorithms that drive same-sex attracted people down 'rabbit holes' of inaccurate online information about 'conversion therapy'. The exponential growth of platform biometrics such as facial and gait recognition software present a new form of potential inclusion, misrecognition, erasure and surveillance of diverse LGBTQ+ expression (Wang and Kosinski

2018), for people of colour and for women (Hao 2020). These tactics have created a situation where algorithms can be seen to intervene in the lives of LGBTQ+ people, and prey on and annihilate LGBTQ+ identity, as they gather information that can be used against LGBTQ+ people.

Networked, online bias-motivated conduct is further manifested in algorithmically driven 'hate raids' on Amazon-owned streaming platform Twitch, that 'spew racist, sexist, and homophobic language and content' (*Twitch Interactive Inc* v *CruzzControl, CreatineOverdose* [2021, p 2]) through bot-powered fake accounts that spam hateful messages (Grayson 2021). At the same time, hate raids exemplify the networked nature of identity formation between platforms and technologies that go beyond the intentions of designers and users. For example,

> [t]he damage might be done on Twitch [or other platforms], but it is organized on chat platforms like Discord (a Voice over Internet Protocol and instant messaging social platform) and signal-boosted (sharing another person's online content with one's own followers or friends on social media to raise awareness of an issue or event) on YouTube and far-right-friendly video sites like BitChute [a UK-based video hosting service known for hosting conspiracy theorists and condoning hate speech]. (Grayson 2021, np)

As such, responses to viral hate need to be addressed systematically, and require timely, coordinated action from digital platforms and traditional news media.

The contagion of ambiguity

Consumers and voters are ambivalent about big tech and government appropriation of surplus information about their behaviour (Zuboff 2019) – the uneasy compromise between convenience and consent when responsibility for basic protections is absent. Slow responses from digital platforms to claims of hateful conduct against LGBTQ+ and other forms of diverse expression support claims of the ambivalence of the technocracy towards addressing representational harms (Chan 2022). This ambiguity in turn amplifies representational harms against politically vulnerable communities through speculation that drives algorithmic predation – a form of structural violence that can limit full realization of somatic and mental potential (Galtung 1969, p 167). For example, when right-wing commentator Tim Pool in July 2022 falsely claimed that the LGBTQ+ community had been 'taken over' by paedophiles, the YouTube video remained up nearly a week later, having accumulated more than a quarter of a million views (Gingerich 2022).

Delays in addressing representational harms on digital platforms, in turn generate speculation online about what the platform should or should not be doing to moderate the harm. That engagement is subsequently amplified by algorithmic intervention, which then amplifies representational harms against LGBTQ+ peoples, and which can be grounded in categories of stigmatic sexual conduct. The latest annual EU review of online platforms' compliance with the EU's code of disinformation bears this out – TikTok is the only online platform to have improved on the timely removal of hate speech (Chan 2022). As a consequence, trust is in short supply. At the same time, can it be said that digital platforms are committed to LGBTQ+ diversity and inclusion by broadening online gender identification options, while still configuring users into a binary system of male or female at the database level (Bivens 2017)?

The contradictions are clear when these claims are made by unstable digital platforms that are yet to strike the right balance between profit and safety. They promise connectivity and convenience while espousing inclusion and diversity, and benefit from the visibility of participation in LGBTQ+ events such as pride parades. But on the platforms, LGBTQ+ people and communities find themselves in the crosshairs of bigotry so well known to the politically vulnerable. An additional complication is that hate groups are being removed from popular social media platforms, moving their communications into encrypted chatrooms, making it harder to track them (The Southern Poverty Law Center 2020b).

Compounding these problems is a loss of trust in news media and two-party politics, arguably driven by partisan news media framing that does not resonate with the range of lived experiences shared and compared on social media platforms (Lee et al 2022). At the same time, the diversification of digital media can expose 'flaktivism' – the notion that politically insecure groups such as LGBTQ+ are granted visibility in news media to the extent that they can support the status quo through providing false balance – while those media companies profit from the structural disadvantage of the status quo, and at the same time seem progressive (Corey 2019, see also Chomsky and Herman 1988). Proactive dissemination of misinformation through cable news channels in the US and Australia, and big tech funding of news media outlets, further blur the lines of responsibility for perpetuating representational harms against LGBTQ+ expression across platforms (Meade 2021).

Jurisdictions not bound by unqualified US free-speech protections, including Australia, India, the UK and the EU, are regulating digital platforms in response to the inadequate protections provided by those US and other platforms, such as ByteDance, the Chinese owner of TikTok. In doing so, they recognize to some extent that a 'marketplace of ideas', which perpetuates structural bias through algorithmic intervention, has reduced the capacity to reason. Other motives include representing the vested interests of news media that have yet to claw back the advertising revenue lost to digital platforms.

Digiqueer resistance

Atomized regulatory and litigious action against big tech companies, represents the varied experience of the digiqueer across jurisdictions in response to inadequate protections against discrimination through the hybrid media ecosystem. In the face of these threats, LGBTQ+ community organizing through social media has taken on greater importance. It is here that 'algorithmic representational harms' are resisted to combat 'algorithmic symbolic annihilation' – algorithms that further 'normative and reductive understandings of phenomena and identities, rendering some invisible and marginalized' (Karizat et al 2021, p 3).

For as digital anthropologist Mary L. Gray has noted, 'AI (artificial intelligence) can tell us some things, about modelling, about the world we live in. And then it's up to us to say; I want the world to look different. I want to queer it up!' (Wareham, 2021). She suggests that one way to do this is to define a metric through qualitative insights; that ethnography is critical to understanding the contexts that shape aggregated data (Weber, 2020). To qualitative researchers this will not seem a novel approach. Yet, as the examples noted in this book show, with the march of technological essentialism, and emphasis on 'big data', nuance can be lost, and opportunities for targeted interventions missed.

Kafer and Grinberg (2019) see potential in 'transforming current logics of state security and global power to magnify minoritarian life' through 'queer surveillance': the queer defining of normative modes of 'embodiment, risk and disposability' on, and in, queer terms (Kafer and Grinberg 2019, p 592). In doing so, they 'seek to expand the ways in which gender and sexuality intersect with other marginalized identity categories within the dominant logics of surveillance' (Kafer and Grinberg 2019, p. 592). As such, this book, while focusing on representational harms against LGBTQ+, could apply to other segments of minoritarian life that need to work hard to fight off majoritarian tyranny.

Some ways in which digiqueer citizens are queering it up represent continuity with the use of predigital concepts such as closets, outness, authenticity and safe spaces to define LGBTQ+ negotiations of sexuality (Robards et al 2021). At the same time, 'impression management practices – privacy settings, with child 'grooming'. This is in addition to debate-related stress about legislative proposals such as surveys on same-sex marriage, and the potential manifestation of homophobia as a symptom of masculine gender role discrepancy stress. The argument is made for more focus on LGBTQ+ macroeconomic agency as a tactic to mitigate representational harms.

Chapter 5 provides a snapshot of the organizing strategies and tactics that digiqueers can draw from in their fight against representational harms. This includes policy and participatory advocacy, reform efforts, coalition building, pride as economic and social capital, information campaigning, and monitoring. Examples include digital rituals of LGBTQ+ organizing through hashtag activism, crowdfunding advocacy, philanthropy through non-fungible tokens, and the broader commodification of LGBTQ+ identity through ecommerce. Emphasizing the importance of queer knowledge production in the fight for recognition, the chapter connects the gay and lesbian political organizing of the late 1960s and subsequent decades to the neoliberal marketization, professionalization, and individualization of political problems and their solutions in late capitalism. The chapter synthesizes practitioner and academic literature on LGBTQ+ organizing in the pracademic tradition.

Chapter 6, the conclusion, situates the issues faced by the digiqueer within a broader context of the ongoing geopolitical and regulatory instability of digital social life, and the vulnerability of LGBTQ+ communities' political and social status. The chapter asks three key questions about the future balance between the rights of the digiqueer citizen and the obligations of states and corporations: (1) How will LGBTQ+ communities document, evaluate and disseminate their legal, political, and economic capital in response to representational harms? (2) How will big-tech companies respond to the 'techlash', which includes growing calls for regulation of digital platforms, and litigation that has found digital platforms responsible for representational harms such as defamatory content once made aware of it? (3) How will artificial intelligence such as ChatGPT perpetuate and ameliorate the structural biases against pre-digital LGBTQ+ expression through algorithmic discrimination, and responses to that discrimination noted throughout this book? (4) How will LGBTQ+ expression be impacted by information warfare in the grey zone − the space in between peace and war in which state and non-state actors engage in competition − as threats from digital technologies outside of physical war zones increase?

Conclusion

This chapter has summarized the breadth of representational harms facing diverse LGBTQ+ expression and the consequences of stigma for LGBTQ+ agency. In doing so, it has made the connection between these harms, and the broader political, economic and technological context within which they can proliferate. The case studies in the chapter show how debates over sexuality, gender, procreation, religion, and anti-LGBTQ+ extremism through the hybrid media ecosystem, intersect and impact negotiations of diverse sexual and gender identity. It is within this context that the digiqueer citizen fights for representation and recognition through resistance to stigma-derived norms that persist through a hate feedback loop. Many of the representational harms noted in this chapter, and throughout the book, are generated by cultural and technological contexts from the US. Yet these problems remain very much a concern in any jurisdiction where those platforms operate. Ongoing failure of digital platforms to self-regulate to the satisfaction of users and governments, has prompted regulation of big tech in Australia, the UK, the EU and India. However, given the ambivalence of technocracy to many LGBTQ+ rights-based claims, addressing information warfare against LGBTQ+ peoples will take ongoing organizing and vigilance by LGBTQ+ individuals and communities across the globe.

TWO

The Digiqueer Fight Against Algorithmic Governance

Introduction

The sorting of populations into measurable types for security and profit through surveillance technologies has amplified the pre-digital fault lines of anti-LGBTQ+ stigma, reinforcing aspects of the hierarchy of human value. As noted in Chapter 1, algorithmically filtered, discriminatory depictions can reinforce the subordination of a group based on identity, including stereotyping, recognition, denigration and underrepresentation (Mehrabi et al 2021). Platform biometrics such as facial and gait recognition software can be the basis for unlawful discrimination based on ethnicity, race, national origin, gender and other characteristics (United Nations General Assembly, 2019). Artificial intelligence extracts patterns from digital information that contests Western liberal notions of consent and privacy, and is only as reliable as its source information.

Shifting norms on consent have 'blurred' through data accrual on sexual identity and government aggregation of social media data with other available databases (Shephard 2016). The appropriation of digital human experience has 'redistributed' privacy (Zuboff 2019). As a consequence, algorithmic intervention, and the adoption of 'neuroliberal' approaches to behaviour modification – a combination of neoliberal principles with policy initiatives derived from insights in the behavioural sciences (Whitehead et al 2019) – have further justified the erosion of standards of truth and trust in democratic institutions by ostensibly supporting liberal orthodoxies of freedom, while adopting 'novel cognitive strategies, emotions, and pre-cognitive affects as a way of securing preferred forms of social conduct' (Whitehead et al 2019, p 633).

The expropriation of critical human rights has been argued as an overthrow of people's sovereignty and a central tenet of 'surveillance capitalism' – '[a] new economic order that claims human experience as free raw materials for hidden commercial practices of extraction, prediction, and sales' (Zuboff 2019, p vi). Simply put, algorithmic governance, and neuroliberal approaches to behavioural modification, can commodify questionably sourced user-generated data without commensurate investment in strategies to mitigate the social costs of the biases it might generate, and/or perpetuate. It is within this context that the digiqueer citizen must address the intact social origins of stigma, despite the decriminalization of same-sex conduct in a growing number of jurisdictions, the expansion of legitimate categories of vulnerability enshrined in anti-discrimination law (Solanke 2017), and progress made on marriage equality.

This chapter revisits the analytical value of capitalism in the study of social movements and collective identity (Valocchi 2017, p 315). The chapter integrates research into surveillance capitalism and algorithmic governance to consider the impact of the mutual constitution of the corporate–government– digiqueer identity through the hybrid media ecosystem. In doing so, it connects historical and theoretical perspectives on the social consequences of representational harms with the legal, technical and economic infrastructures mediating new forms of identity practices (Phillips and Cunningham 2007).

In considering these issues, the chapter responds to a range of questions: How are the organizing principles of identity-based rights movements evolving with the use of digital media surveillance technology? How might algorithmic aggregates perpetuate a range of representational harms against LGBTQ+ expression, conduct and relationship rights? Will (mis)information capital continue to amplify tribalism at the expense of institutional authority, and how will institutions secure their authority? LGBTQ+ resistance to algorithmic representational harms is one consequence of the ambiguities of surveillance capitalism. However, this resistance reflects the investment required by such communities to secure basic protections that the general population might take for granted.

The chapter applies Castells' (2010) identity framework for the network society and its corresponding forms of socialization, mobilization and political participation. The analysis shows that algorithmic biases and bigotry amplified through the hybrid media ecosystem, in many ways keep LGBTQ+ organizing in the 'digital' trenches as a resistance identity. At the same time, the use of LGBTQ+ political, economic, and social capital through episodic LGBTQ+ campaigns/projects on issues such as same-sex marriage, and adoption rights, can expand the representation of LGBTQ+ identity beyond categorizations of sexual conduct.

Castells' identity framework has three organizing categories:

1. A 'legitimizing' identity that consists of the dominant institutions of society who extend and rationalize their domination through social actors such as churches, parties, unions and civic associations but which also fits with various theories of nationalism;
2. A 'resistance' identity generated by those actors who are in positions or conditions devalued and/or stigmatized by the logic of domination, and who thus build 'trenches' of resistance, such as the invocation of identity politics to address incommensurate criminal justice institutional responses to discrimination against vulnerable populations, with LGBTQ+ communities the relevant example scrutinized in this book; and
3. A 'project' identity – social actors who use the cultural materials available to them to build a new identity that redefines their position in society and, by so doing, seek the transformation of the overall social structure, such as

feminists in their critique of patriarchy that challenges the entire structure of production, reproduction, sexuality and personality on which societies have been historically based (Castells 2010, p 8).

The tensions between these three identities reflect class-based inequalities, grievances, differing class-inflected categories, and capacities for resistance, and the capitalist cultural values of freedom, rights, liberty and property (Valocchi 2017). For the digiqueer, these inequalities continue through legal and medical stigma that can limit opportunity. At the same time, algorithmic governance has exposed the outcomes of classification, while keeping the reasoning and responsibility for the decisions that drive classification ambiguous.

The incapacity or unwillingness of governments, big tech, and other corporations to secure the basic privacy protections necessary to secure one's digital identity speak to Castells' evocation of the traditional institutions and organizations of civil society – legitimizing identities – that were built around the democratic state and around the social contract of labour and capital, as 'large empty shells'. These identities, and their institutions, are 'decreasingly able to relate to people's lives and values in most societies', and 'are so distant from the structure and processes that really matter that they appear to most people as a sarcastic grimace on the new face of history' (Castells 2010, p 420). The recent prominence of high-profile cases of whistleblowing over unauthorized capture or use of data (Rev.com 2021), and major data breaches in Australia, evoke this sarcastic grimace.

Anti-LGBTQ+ group invocation of a resistance identity through hybrid networks by religious conservatives, right-wing nationalist extremists, and some politicians, is indicative of their real and/or perceived transition from legitimizing identities to resistance identities. This resistance is occurring amid the broader rise of populism based on geographic identity, and in conjunction with the amorphous tribalism of digital networks and globalization (Castells 2010). This is exemplified in the confluence of libertarian and extremist messaging within the Alternative Influence Network (AIN) on YouTube that can radicalize, and which can include anti-LGBTQ+ hate. The next section grounds digiqueer expression in historical narratives of capitalism as a system of economic and political power. The chapter then details the relationship between surveillance capitalism and the negotiation of digiqueer identity through technologies such as platform biometrics, and 'queer surveillance'. The chapter provides a summary of recent approaches to regulating the hybrid media ecosystem to combat representational harms.

Capitalism and the digiqueer citizen

D'Emilio (1983/2007) argued that the analytical value of capitalism to the study of gay and lesbian social movements is its capacity to 'affect our perception of identity, our formulation of political goals, and our decisions about strategy' (d'Emilio 1983/2007, p 256). Valocchi has more recently argued that '[r]ather than viewing gay identity and the movement through the prism of resources, opportunities, social networks and social construction', that 'these processes are best subsumed under the broader rubric of the capitalist political economy' (Valocchi 2017, p 315). Aspects of the current negotiation of LGBTQ+ representation and resources though the hybrid media ecosystem, bear these two perspectives out. However, the expropriation of critical human rights through the capture of behavioural surplus without consent, and breaches of privacy, sit uneasily with the Western capitalist priority of legal protection of property. At the same time, online and in-person hate have increased in recent years in this context, despite the decriminalization of same-sex conduct in a growing number of jurisdictions, legal protections provided through anti-discrimination law (Solanke 2017), and progress made on marriage equality. Furthermore, this book provides an overview of current issues on the relationship between identity, digital media technology and LGBTQ+ agency. As such, it very much focuses on the granularity around organizing that supports Valocchi's broader view.

Bearing these points in mind, how has capitalism been conceptualized in relation to the development of LGBTQ+ identity over time, and what contribution can surveillance capitalism make to articulating the issues facing the digiqueer?

D'Emilio argues that industrial capitalism enabled the development of lesbian and gay identities through material independence from the confines of the procreative family unit that sustained future generations (d'Emilio 1983/2007). At the same time, he noted that 'the ideology of capitalist society has enshrined the family as the source of love, affection, and emotional security, the place where our need for stable, intimate human relationships is satisfied' (d'Emilio 1983/2007, p 255). The broadening of acceptance of 'rainbow families' through incorporating LGBTQ+ peoples under the procreative umbrella, and through positive, popular representation of those demographics, speaks to this enshrinement and its potential to mitigate heterosexism and homophobia, and at the same time, for rainbow families to potentially become a target for anti-LGBTQ+ hate.

Valocchi (2017) has examined the ways in which capitalism as a system of economic and political purchase has changed over the course of the 20th and 21st centuries, and how those changes have affected the gay and lesbian movement, and the collective identity constructed by the movement. He argues that different kinds of capitalism have yielded different dominant understandings of gay identity held by the movement over its 70-year history. For example, 'reform capitalism' created a psychiatric gay identity. The harmful legacy of reform capitalism is still evident under the auspices of 'sexual orientation, gender identity or gender expression change efforts' (SOGIECE; otherwise known as 'conversion therapy' or 'ex-gay therapy'). The commodification of this stigmatization might still involve investment in products such as 'electroshock aversion therapy' and 'chemical aversion therapy', 'internment in clinics or camps', 'exorcism and spiritual/miracle cures' (ILGA World 2020a, p 5) and funding schemes, as well as biomedical ideas and institutions.

'Social contract capitalism' created a personal 'out' minority gay identity; 'Capitalism-in-crisis', through deindustrialization and economic insecurity, created a de-centred and contested gay identity, broadening class, gender, and racial intersections among gays and lesbians, and the meaning of gay identity (Valocchi 2017). This broadening, to some extent, is reflected in the current proliferation of queer identity. 'Neoliberal capitalism' created a domesticated and consumerist gay identity (Valocchi 2017), conceptualized in Duggan's (2002) 'new homonormativity' of sexual politics; a discourse that normalizes and assimilates certain kinds of sexual orientation and gender identity into mainstream culture through domesticity and consumption.

In terms of 21st century neoliberal capitalists working within the technocracy, Valocchi (2017, p 316) argues that they have 'generated a class fraction of finance and digital capitalists' that has given dominant social movement organizations tremendous economic resources to build national professional organizations, in the US in particular. As such, in the past century, LGBTQ+ people have built identities in various ways as a counter-culture, by claiming rights, and so on. Such resources have enabled these organizations to refashion a minority identity into a domesticated 'post-gay' identity (Ghaziani 2008, pp 99–100; Altman, 1971/2012), which emphasizes cultural sameness and equal rights.

The wider impacts of capitalist technocracy and the recent resurgence in representational harms have complicated the notion of the 'post-gay' identity, and demanded LGBTQ+ mobilization to defend unsettled territory. Namely backlash to same-sex marriage (in Australia and the US), and conflation of drag performance not only with child 'groomer' rhetoric, but with 'adult' performance. This necessity also speaks to aspects of Castells' (2010) segmentation of identity, and its mobilizing power in relation to capital in informational democracies through digital networks. One recent example is the mobilizing of drag communities to legitimize Drag Queen Storytime (DQS) – a childhood literacy programme that involves drag queens reading to children in public spaces such as libraries – through the establishment of Drag Queen Story Hour as a non-profit organization (Drag Queen Story Hour, 2020): arguably, a form of resistance identity to protect the expression of gender fluidity harnessed through digital networks (see Chapter 3 in this volume). It is to further analysis of the mutual constitution of the corporate–government–digiqueer identity through digital networks and its impact on LGBTQ+ negotiation of rights, recognition and resources, that we now turn.

Owning sexual identity in technocratic times

As Lyon and others have noted (Gandy 1993, Lyon 2003), surveillance sorts populations through processes of identification and classification to control access to resources and information. As such, surveillance is a process of assignation (Crampton 2019). As Foucault (1981, p 146) made clear, sexological classification systems based on statistical averages developed a standard against which deviance could be measured, and justified the moral arguments for regulation of that deviance through political operations, economic interventions and ideological campaigns for raising standards of morality and responsibility. As Kafer and Grinberg have succinctly put it, '[d]eviations from the [sexological] norm can be framed as dangerous to state functions and corporate initiatives' (Kafer and Grinberg, p 592), while serving a purpose through the stigmatization of marginal groups such as LGBTQ+ as a form of coercion, and as seen through anti-gay legislation in Russia.

Assigning worth or risk through sorting has real effects on people's life chances and makes surveillance not just a matter of personal privacy, but of social justice (Lyon 2003). What those who control the information from the assignation do with it impacts the right to digital self-determination (Zuboff 2019), and related concerns of freedom of expression and freedom from discrimination. In the algorithmic context, Kiat uses the term 'allocational harms' to define unfair allocation of opportunities or resources due to algorithmic intervention (Kiat n.d.). Debates over ownership of identity occur in the broader context of the shared interests between fledgling surveillance capitalists and state intelligence agencies. Tech corporations have been tenacious in defending their new territories (Zuboff, 2019) through resistance to government regulation, and continued slowness in addressing online representational harms.

The confluence of surveillance capitalism and algorithmic governance raises questions about ownership of sexual identity and the mutually constituted relationship between identification and identity through hybrid media. This blurring is in tension with legal principles that seek to objectively define the responsibility of the individual, and neoliberal mantras that have undermined the legitimacy of democratic institutions.

This is because notions of blurred consent and redistributed privacy under the auspices of premarket, liberal economic freedoms evoke social welfarist approaches to individual agency. These communitarian principles contradict claims of liberal economic freedom espoused by technocrats, and are justified through digital essentialist arguments from behavioural modification proponents. Arguments that critics label in terms of 'computational essentialism', 'attribute-based exclusion', (van Nuenen et al 2022) and 'algorithmic symbolic annihilation' (Karizat et al 2021). They also evoke deterministic, marginalizing narratives from bio-social positivist criminology that have been used to stigmatize difference.

Pseudo-scientific theories such as phrenology, which were part of the history of pathologizing deviation through the typification of individual characteristics (Gates 2011), continue through poorly justified attempts to evaluate machine learning capacity to infer the validity of physiognomy in determining criminality (Wu and Zhang 2016). At the same time, the controversial use of facial recognition software to determine sexual identity, shows there is still novelty in representations of same-sex attraction (Wang and Kosinski 2018) that prioritize the physical over other dimensions of identity.

The appropriation by surveillance capitalists of behavioural surplus – appropriated human experience – is inextricably linked with geopolitical forces through the diminution of privacy protections in the US in response to the 9/11 attacks under the auspices of national security threats. Kafer and Grinberg (2019, p 596) have argued that in the post-9/11 moment, the enumerative function of surveillance was 'exacerbated by the operative logics of global telecommunications and military planning', which have been 'exceedingly apparent within the warped temporalities of pre-emption'.

Pre-emptive control converts potential futures of feelings of fear, suspicion and insecurity 'into a material causality of the present' (Kafer and Grinberg 2019, p 596). The perception of risks and the invocation of war rhetoric in such contexts can signify 'the transition from a routine concern to a state of emergency' (Bittner 1970, p 48), which does not allow for patient study. Nor is there any need to show the certainty of the impending risk nor 'estimate its likelihood with precision' (Bittner 1970, p 48). Inaccurate and inflammatory 'gays as groomers' rhetoric, and the expansive range of reasons why protestors object to DQS events, reflect the invocation of a 'sexual emergency' (see Berlant in Chapter 3) as an essential tactic of hate in information warfare against LGBTQ+ expression.

Telecommunications *as* military planning speaks to the co-option of LGBTQ+ sexual identity as a component of information warfare predicated on the normalization of exclusion. A product of this environment is that the state of emergency generated through angertainment might be focused on bigoted victims – such as religious conservatives and right-wing extremists. At the same time, the ambivalence of digital platforms in addressing representational harms downplays the actual harms that are occurring through the manifestation of online sentiment into in-person attacks (Williams et al 2020), and the other way around. Wiedlitzka et al (2021) have called the latter phenomenon 'compound retaliation' – media and social media dissemination of offline acts of hate that compound already tense intergroup hostilities, and which can provide further permission for those to express hatred online (Wiedlitzka et al 2021). The next section analyses the relationship between identity formation, blurred consent, and the redistribution of privacy, as platform biometrics and emotional recognition technologies bring the surveillance of the digiqueer citizen into full fruition (Crampton, 2019).

Platform biometrics and the uneasy compromise

Use of facial recognition software by a range of stakeholders raises deeper questions about the ownership of identity, the right to self-representation, and the necessity to interrogate the logic in action of surveillance capitalism that looks beyond the technological (Zuboff 2019). The tension between corporate interests, government legitimacy, and LGBTQ+ agency, is reflected in the contested uses and decision-making processes around big-tech manufacture of platform biometrics.

As Crampton (2019) has noted, digital surveillance is not new. However, platform biometrics and emotional recognition technologies that measure behavioural and physical characteristics such as facial expressions, gait, galvanic skin response, and palm or iris patterns, mark a shift from 'surveillance as epistemology (what is seen is known) to surveillance as ontology (what is "seen as" comes into being)' (Crampton 2019, p 61). Given the likelihood of 'continued field deployment of biometrics, careful disambiguation of their social impacts needs to be parsed out' (Crampton 2019, p 61). This is especially the case with their use by government agencies such as law enforcers, and corporations, without informed consent.

The inaccuracy of platform biometrics is reflected in a freedom of information campaign by Big Brother Watch in the UK that revealed that facial recognition technology used by London's Metropolitan Police had wrongly identified innocent people 98 per cent of the time (Big Brother Watch 2018). Affect recognition seeks to infer a person's feelings, emotions or intentions from facial expressions, based on highly questionable (United Nations General Assembly 2019) and opaque classification systems (Crampton 2019).

Aspects of the sarcastic grimace are further reflected in New York-based company Clearview AI scraping Australians' biometric information from the internet without consent and disclosing it through a facial recognition tool. The Australian Federal Police's failure to comply with its privacy obligations by using Clearview AI's tool on a trial basis between November 2019 and January 2020 (Office of the Australian Information Commissioner 2021) further undermines trust in institutions and justifies civilian scepticism.

Amazon, Microsoft and other manufacturers have backed away from selling facial recognition software to law enforcement agencies until protections are secured. IBM have ceased production of facial recognition altogether. Given persistent contention over consent and privacy on digital platforms, and related questions about government and big-tech responsibility and accountability, the cause for pause is warranted. In the policing context, identity alignment can enhance the legitimization of police performance through the extent to which a social group can justify police actions as lawful (Bradford 2014, Bradford et al 2017). Policing agencies adopting contested technologies without informed consent will likely reinforce mistrust in vulnerable communities.

Activist experimentation with the use of facial recognition software to identify police officers who might conceal their faces or name badges during public protests (Hill 2020) is indicative of the ongoing tensions between police surveillance through an ever-growing range of cameras and hierarchical sousveillance – the watching of authority from below with political or legal intent (Bakir et al 2017). As such, the promise of pervasive cell-phone camera hierarchical sousveillance 'has been weaponized against people as they become potentially another data source for surveillance' (Gregory 2019, p 379). In such contexts, platform biometrics promise not only to connect geographically distant actors through the networked nature of the hybrid media ecosystem, but to curate new forms of value (Crampton 2019) for state actors and activists.

A more pernicious influence of microtargeting – direct marketing datamining techniques that involve predictive marketing segmentation – is discrimination by employers through algorithmic intervention (Angwin et al 2017). This form of discrimination is palpable in jurisdictions where 'the question of dis/allowing exemptions on religious grounds from laws aimed at protecting LGBT people from discrimination in the provision of services and employment' (Richardson 2018, p 33) is yet to be settled (Ball et al 2019).

There is a general unease about the capacity or interest of governments, digital platforms, and other corporations to protect privacy rights or more tightly enforce consent. At the same time, some audiences see the compromising of those rights as a fair trade for participation in 'economic' surveillance that might benefit the consumer, or what Jansson (2015, p 81) has called interveillance, 'non-hierarchical and non-systematic monitoring practices' as part of everyday life underpinned by 'everyday mutual sharing and disclosure of private information'. This emphasizes the 'continuously contested and socially moulded nature of mediatization' (Jansson 2015, p 82). Interveillance, such as access to photographs through drivers' licence databases, has set the scene for ongoing debate over the (co)ownership of digital identity between individuals, tech companies, and governments (Lauder 2015).

Blurred consent and the redistribution of privacy might on balance be acceptable for some consumers if they can also use facial recognition software to curate their own photographs, and because of the convenience of biometric authentication. The mundane sorting of personal images exemplifies the integrated and mutually constituted nature of identity between individuals, corporations and government. This is despite the exposure of the unauthorized use of personal data for computational politics, notable in the Facebook–Cambridge Analytica scandal (Afriat et al 2021).

This context speaks not only to the identity-forming nature for individuals of background 'relations among machines' (Wood 2021), but also group identity formation through elections (see also *US Dominion, Inc.* v *Fox News Network, LLC* [2021] defamation case that alleges the cable TV network amplified false claims that Dominion voting machines were used to rig the 2020 US presidential election). It also makes plain the unpredictable nature of the 'technicity of technologies': 'the elements of technology that exceed the intentions of its designers and users and which act to create new needs and functions among these users' (Wood 2021, p 629), with unpredictable geopolitical implications. At the same time, conservative attempts at electoral and judicial scale reform that might include actors who seek to marginalize LGBTQ+ peoples are indicative of nostalgia from real and/ or perceived legitimizing identities that base their claims on the necessity to revert to a 'simpler time' imaginary that eschews gender expression beyond the binary, and who invoke 'sexual emergency' rhetoric to push back on LGBTQ+ enfranchisement.

If fair treatment by authority is an organizing principle of social identity, and fair treatment by authority is in turn linked to cooperation (Bradford 2014), then the slipperiness of blurred consent and redistributed privacy results in some form of blind coercion. At the same time, if meaning is socially produced, and 'social comparisons between groups are relevant to an evaluation of a person's social identity' (Miles-Johnson 2016, p 608), then omission through algorithmic governance of some LGBTQ+ peoples is a form of marginalization through lack of recognition.

Queer surveillance

The term 'queer surveillance' has been used to describe 'the power dynamic through which queerness is actualized as the necessary difference that adjudicates the bounds between normative and non-normative modes of embodiment, risk and disposability' (Kafer and Grinberg 2019, p 592). Kafer and Grinberg see the possibility in 'transforming current logics of state security and global power to magnify minoritarian life', and 'seek to expand the ways in which gender and sexuality intersect with other marginalized identity categories within the dominant logics of surveillance' (Kafer and Grinberg 2019, p 592).

Schram has argued that big data analytics have rendered queerness ineffectual firstly through the proscription of identity at the individual level and through the 'feed-forward' processes of consumer analytics that 'have stripped the agency once attributed to the desire that underpinned performative articulations of queer embodiment' (Kafer and Grinberg 2019, p 598). In such contexts, subjects might be left out of the picture because, for example, they have 'gay looking faces', in the same way that 'gay sounding voices' may be stigmatized and marginalized (Fasoli et al 2021). On the digital categorization of transgender people, Beauchamp (2019) has argued that increased surveillance at airports has opened up 'different questions about nonnormative bodies and about bodily anomalies that position them not as fixed, ahistorical, or easily read markers of deviance, but rather as active interpretations that – like the images from AIT [Advanced Imaging Technology] scanners themselves – can shift according to context' (Beauchamp 2019, p 77).

Considering these perspectives on categorization through digital technologies, in what ways does surveillance capitalism contribute to the notion of the 'post-gay' (Altman 1971/2012) through the aggregation and standardization of LGBTQ+ typologies that diminish the spectrum of identity expression that has burgeoned in recent years? Magnet (2011) has argued that non-conforming conventions of gendered grooming and dress are computed as 'biometric system failures' (Magnet 2011, p 48) 'that must be corrected by conforming to the discursive constructs in the software' (Kafer and Grinberg 2019, p 593). This point is made to some extent in the use of facial recognition software to define a less than hirsute 'gay look' (Wang and Kosinski 2018), despite the ubiquity of the hipster beard – gay or straight. Kornstein has noted drag 'as a potent but under-recognized form of informational obfuscation' (Kafer and Grinberg 2019, p 599), which is also an incidental dimension of a resistance identity.

Individual rights-based agency and the subsequent commodification of same-sex and other sex and gender identities is now in a complex relationship with the behavioural surplus generated through digital devices, appropriated by surveillance capitalists. This appropriation challenges liberal and legal notions of privacy, consent and corporate social responsibility. These corporations are also deriving their revenue from behavioural surplus and developing products that can be used to surveil vulnerable populations, which generates ongoing further sources of behavioural surplus that surveillance capitalists seek to appropriate.

This perpetual, mutual constitution of the digital subject, known as the 'data flywheel', has been framed as an act of enlightened self-interest that contributes to ever-growing data accumulation under the auspices of total algorithmic control (Zuboff 2019). The notion of the 'data flywheel' is in turn central to the accumulation and monetization of data from everyday digital media consumption and its storage in 'the cloud' to achieve the 'scalability, flexibility, and cost-efficiency needed for businesses to achieve "self-sustaining momentum"' (Amazon Web Services 2022, np).

As digital platforms such as YouTube mature, the contradictions become clearer between the platform's increasingly cautious rules on 'advertiser-friendly' content, its dynamic financial and algorithmic incentive structure, and its declared values as a platform for open expression (Caplan and Gillespie 2020, p 1). As such, YouTube's hierarchical governance strategy, which offers different sets of rules to different users, different material resources, and 'different procedural protections when content is demonetized' (Caplan and Gillespie 2020, p 1), is problematic from a digital platform that ostensibly supports LGBTQ+ diversity and inclusion.

There are reputational risks to digital platforms, when the details of 'tiered governance are ambiguous or poorly conveyed', as creators can then develop 'their own theories for why their content has been demonetized – which can provide some creators a tactical opportunity to advance politically motivated accusations of bias against the platform', including gay creators (Caplan and Gillespie 2020, p 1). Misinformation through digital platforms has facilitated a broader hybrid media ecosystem that prioritizes conflict, amid reduced journalistic standards.

A profound loss of confidence and trust in democracy (Cameron and McAllister 2019) can in part be attributed to the surveillance capitalist trouncing of Western liberal principles of privacy and consent, and the loss of agency over one's behavioural surplus that is then used to justify behavioural modifications. The 'ambiveillance' integral to the uncertain privacy environment of a digital life; of not knowing if you are being watched and not knowing if it is good (Cascio 2013), generate an ambivalence about agency that is based on this compromise of convenience.

Information warfare from without and within

Surveillance capitalism and the information warfare that has manifested under its auspices are arguably foregrounded in the imprecision of 'actuarial justice' – risk profiling based on aggregates (Feeley and Simon 1994) – that has had a mutually constitutive effect on the broader separation of fundamental principles such as privacy and consent from their legal underpinnings within the 'pre-crime' environment (Zedner 2007). This environment has seen a concurrent diminution of ministerial standards in the US, the UK and Australia that has reduced trust in politicians, the traditional news media and the two-party political system (Cameron and McAllister 2019, Newman et al 2020). At the same time, information warfare has taken on greater currency, both in terms of networked anti-LGBTQ+ hate from religious and extremist groups, and state actors such as Russia.

The conceptualization of information warfare resonates with the range of representational harms challenging LGBTQ+ expression, central to which is an opposition that manufactures an imagined enemy (Papadopoulos 2003). This exclusion is predicated on comparison, and one which has been enhanced through social networks and their concomitant amplification of conflict, while also providing pockets of sanctuary through which to explore diverse sexual and gender identities. The 'looseness' of the technocratic approach noted by Esmark (2020) speaks to the ambiguity of responsibility for the consequences of claims made in traditional news and cable media channels that are subsequently disseminated through social media channels. An extension of the war analogy with ambiguity over information warfare in the hybrid media context is that

> hybrid actors [in the context of hybrid war] blur the usual borders of international politics and operate in the interfaces between external and internal, legal and illegal, and peace and war. The ambiguity is created by combining conventional and unconventional means – disinformation and interference in political debate or elections, critical infrastructure disturbances or attacks, cyber operations, different forms of criminal activities and, finally, an asymmetric use of military means and

warfare. (European Centre of Excellence for Countering Hybrid Threats 2022, np)

The hybrid media ecosystem, with its amplification of misinformation and disinformation, is embedded in the broader 'hybrid action' warfare environment (European Centre of Excellence for Countering Hybrid Threats 2022). The instability of media, not only through the porosity of digital platforms, but also at the organizational level, continues with ongoing diversification and fragmentation. For example, much of the war in Ukraine is conveyed via Telegram. Platforms such as Telegram and Parler that gained currency under the Trump presidency have gone more mainstream, while still harbouring extremist sentiment, including incitement against LGBTQ+ peoples.

In 2021, the Australian government enacted legislation to enable eligible news businesses to bargain individually or collectively with digital platforms over payment for the inclusion of news on the platforms and services (Treasury Laws Amendment (News Media and Digital Platforms Mandatory Bargaining Code) Act 2021). The aim of the mandatory code is 'to help support the sustainability of public interest journalism in Australia' and 'address bargaining power imbalances between digital platforms and Australian news businesses' (Australian Communications and Media Authority 2022, np). Other jurisdictions are contemplating similar legislation. The impact on LGBTQ+ public interest journalism remains to be seen.

In Australia, renewed calls have been made for national guidelines on facial recognition software when it was revealed that major retail chains were capturing the biometric information of their clients through facial recognition and that 76 per cent of consumers did not know this was happening (CHOICE 2022). Those calls reiterate the Australian Human Rights Commission's (2021) call for legislation that expressly protects human rights in the use of technology in decision making that has a legal, or similarly significant effect for individuals, or where there is a high risk to human rights, such as in policing and law enforcement.

In addition to ongoing anti-trust cases in the US, the atomistic regulation of big tech in recent years reflects not only the 'techlash' against big tech in general, and the big-tech 'quintet' in particular (Apple, Amazon, Alphabet, Meta, and Microsoft), but government attempts to restore legitimacy with their constituents. The UK's Age-Appropriate Design Code came into force in September 2021, codifying the UK's obligations under s.123 (1) of the UK Data Protection Act (Data Protection Act 2018). The UK continues to debate its Online Safety Bill. That bill had been criticized for likely falling foul of the free-speech provisions of the European Convention on Human Rights, to which the UK remains a signatory (*The Economist* 2022). Other concerning aspects of the Bill are new communications offences that rely on subjective definitions of psychological harm, vagueness around definitions of terrorism, and police worries that firms could destroy digital evidence of crime by deleting posts (*The Economist* 2022).

The EU's Digital Services Act for the first time provides a common set of rules on intermediaries' obligations and accountability across the single market that will open up new opportunities to provide digital services across borders, while ensuring a high level of protection to all users, no matter where they live in the EU. Together with the Digital Services Act, the Digital Markets Act is one of the centrepieces of the European digital strategy and aims to ensure that large online platforms who act as 'gatekeepers' in digital markets behave in a fair way online (European Commission 2022). India announced rules in February 2021 to regulate social media content that would make Facebook, WhatsApp and others more accountable to legal requests to remove posts and identify original posters of certain messages (Government of India 2021).

The far-right conspiracy theory and fake news website Infowars' founder Alex Jones' second defamation case loss against Sandy Hook victims, in which limits were imposed on speech, but not on the potential earnings off the back of such speech (Lewis 2022), show how broader responses to representational harms though digital platforms resonate in the LGBTQ+ space. A recent defamation case in Australia found YouTube liable as a publisher of user-generated content once it is made aware of the content (*Barilaro* v *Google LLC* [2022] FCA 650). While the judgment involves 'the application of an orthodox principle to a new setting', and is more driven by economics and politics than legal principles (see Rolph in Mason 2022, np), it is one example among many drawn on throughout the book that shows the ways in which civilians and governments are challenging representational harms in general, and in relation to LGBTQ+ expression in particular. That case, however, is likely to have less impact in the US, where Google maintains its immunity from content regulation based on its non-publisher status in in the US Communications Decency Act (*LGBTQ+* v *Google Inc* [2020]), as do all digital platforms in the US.

Jurisdictions such as China, where TikTok owner ByteDance is headquartered (incorporated in the Cayman Islands), present new realms of challenge given China's cultural distance from Western human rights principles. However, given the range of harms generated by Western technocracy, leverage against human rights violations in jurisdictions that do not prioritize those rights emboldens the sarcastic grimace at the geopolitical level. This difference and shift in responses to representational harm facilitated by big tech is reflected in the lengths that journalist Carlos Maza went to have YouTube amend its policies after Maza claimed that he had been harassed by Steven Crowder, a conservative pundit, who repeatedly used homophobic slurs against Maza on YouTube (Alexander 2020). YouTube's response included the demonetizing of Crowder's YouTube account, and in which YouTube noted the frequency of the homophobic and racist slurs against Maza as part of the rationale for demonetization (Spangler 2019). Crowder has since litigated against Facebook and YouTube.

Reflecting elements of the atomization and fragmentation of digital media, Esmark characterizes the new technocratic approach to governance not as 'a fixed system of thought or coherent political programme, but a loosely connected set of ideas and material practices used across the globe, albeit with a clear slant towards advanced liberal democracies' (Esmark 2020, p 13). The nature of the loosely connected speaks to the lack of clarity inherent in notions of blurred consent, redistributed privacy and unqualified invocations of national security that might have some correlation with unqualified invocations of freedom of speech that perpetuate ongoing violence against LGBTQ+ communities through sexual emergencies.

Conclusion

The intersection of technology, pre-emptive risk, and identity that informs surveillance capitalism, is challenging Western liberal notions of individuality and equality that have driven identity politics for decades. The curation of LGBTQ+ expression though sorting populations into measurable types for security and profit through surveillance technologies presents threats and opportunities to those individuals and groups. More pernicious is the loss of individual agency over behavioural surplus, feeding the pursuit of total control over the individual through algorithmic governance that might diminish the scope for LGBTQ+ expression, conduct and relationship rights. As such, visibility has become a double-edged sword for communities who have gained recognition through identity politics, but whose visibility remains a potential target for violence. Within this watchful context of surveillance and sousveillance, the possibilities of latent, hierarchical sousveillance to counter the nefarious use of digital media technology, remain unknown, and will vary by jurisdiction. But it is likely to be prevalent where recreation, protest and/or disadvantage in public spaces clusters, and where policing intersects with populations who use such spaces for celebration, protest or shelter. As dystopic as invocations of total surveillance are, the ongoing necessity is now is to take as much ownership over one's identity as possible, while navigating the unstable and potentially violent ideological minefield that is online participation. The next chapter analyses the information warfare confronting Drag Queen Story Time organizers, presenters, and audiences, as they navigate that minefield.

THREE

Information Warfare Against Drag Queen Storytime

Introduction

Drag Queen Storytime (DQS) childhood literacy events became a focus of networked, hybrid hateful conduct between 2018 and 2020 in the US, with related conduct and commentary in Australia and the UK. This outrage occurred within a broader rise in reported 'hate crime', notable in the US (Edwards and Rushin 2018) and in England and Wales (Williams et al 2020). That rise occurred within a polarization of politics that encouraged the online growth of partisan agendas, misinformation driven by domestic politicians (Newman et al 2019), and permissiveness by digital platforms of hateful conduct (Hern 2020, Roose 2020). At the same time, violent domestic extremism became an increasing concern in the US (US Department of Homeland Security 2020), the UK (Sengupta 2020), and Australia (Greene 2020). Concurrently, drag performance through television programmes such as RuPaul's Drag Race have popularized drag beyond niche audiences.

During June 2022 – Pride month in the US and many other jurisdictions – in-person and online protests to DQS events have continued amid the growth of alt-right movements, some of which are now classified as extremist groups. These include the Proud Boys and the Three Percenters (Combating Terrorism Center at West Point 2021). The global nature of these networks is reflected in the postponement of a drag event in Melbourne in December 2022 because of threats from suspected Neo-Nazi and Proud Boys members (Thomas 2022). These more recent protests against DQS events have occurred within a sharpened framing of the conflation of male same-sex attraction with threats to children through 'gays as child groomers' rhetoric (Tiffany 2022).

This chapter analyses the mutual constitution of online representational harms against DQS childhood literacy events and its manifestation in in-person hateful conduct, and the other way around.[1] The chapter documents the range of direct and indirect violence used to censor the gender-fluid expression of DQS, which include vilification, harassment, intimidation, alleged assault and malicious property damage; vexatious litigation, antagonistic legislative proposals that restrict resourcing of public libraries, the threatening of librarians with prison terms, and the criminalization of drag peformance in Tennessee (amid a wave of anti-LGBTQ+ legislation in the US).

In doing so, the chapter contributes to a growing body of literature that conceptualizes the link between men's rights activist group subcultures within the broader 'manosphere', and how they may encourage and propagate violence (Nicholas and Agius 2018, Jones et al 2020). Analysis of news media, case law, and general public discourse on bias-motivated hateful conduct against DQS events emphasizes the invocation of recursive medico-legal and pseudo-scientific stigma of same-sex attraction and gender fluidity to chill LGBTQ+ expression. And the amplificatory capacity of social media networks to engender hateful conduct.

The chapter analyses the broader implications of hateful conduct given the limits of criminal law in the US (and other Western liberal democracies such as the UK and Australia) in addressing the translation of online hate speech into bias-motivated in-person hateful conduct. In the US, these limits are often defined through the unqualified invocation of freedom of speech protections. The chapter argues that notions of sexual purity linked to nationhood drive networked hate by Christian groups and far-right extremists and its intersection with manosphere groups to censor diverse sexual orientation and gender expression.

In doing so, the chapter critically analyses the amplification of representational harms against LGBTQ+ people through digital media and their intersection, particularly in the US, with Christian righteousness and right-wing ideology through a censorious 'hate feedback loop' (Bjork-James 2019).

The chapter firstly details examples of networked hate against DQS and responses to this hate. It then goes on to define hateful conduct in the US, the UK, and Australia, and recent proposals from the EU to protect LGBTQ+ peoples from hate. The chapter then analyses the interrelationship between sexuality, Christianity and nationalism, before considering the ongoing invocation of the anti-LGBTQ+ hate feedback loop as a form of information warfare.

Drag Queen Storytime, recursive hate and extremism

Drag Queen Storytime is an umbrella term for childhood literacy programmes that combine the promotion of reading and drag performance to create 'diverse, accessible, and cultural inclusive family programming where kids can express their authentic selves and become bright lights of change in their communities' (Drag Queen Story Hour 2020, np). DQS events originated in a Drag Queen Story Hour initiative in San Francisco in 2015. Drag Queen Story Hour has since been established as a non-profit organization (Drag Queen Story Hour 2020). Many uncontentious DQS events were held in the US between 2015 and 2017. However, by late 2018, as the popularity and visibility of DQS grew, it had become a rapidly growing area of controversy (Stone 2018a).

Protest against DQS differs from other forms of censorship as its main target is not specific book titles nor specific speakers, but the method in which stories are presented to children (Stone 2018a): drag queens reading to children rather than a range of other diverse presenters that collectively might represent a community. Controversy over DQS has occurred within a generally divisive public discourse about gender, permissiveness of hateful speech online (Hern 2020, Roose 2020), and the glorification of violence on social media that reached its zenith with the US Capitol riot on 6 January 2021 (Dwoskin and Timberg 2021). It is notable that the first conviction of a protester at the riot is a member of the Three Percenters (*United States* v *Reffitt* [2022]), who have targeted DQS events (Stone 2019c).

Conservative Christian and far-right counter-movements have allegedly sought to capitalize on the so-called 'Trump effect' (Edwards and Rushin 2018), the notion that the divisive rhetoric used by Donald Trump during the 2016 US presidential campaign, and throughout his term, amplified through his use of social media, would embolden hate crime perpetrators, thereby contributing to more hate crimes. The broader impact of the 'Trump effect' saw groups that vilify the LGBTQ+ community represent the fastest-growing sector among hate groups in 2019 – expanding from 49 in 2018 to 70 in 2019, a nearly 43 per cent increase (Southern Poverty Law Center 2020b).[2] Since the US Capitol riot in January 2021, some groups involved in the insurrection have increased in size, with Proud Boys chapters growing from 43 in 2020 to 72 in 2022 (Bernstein and Marritz 2022).[3]

Amid the rise in extremism, researchers have established 'a general temporal and spatial association between online hate speech targeting race and religion and offline racially and religiously aggravated crimes independent of "trigger" events', such as terror attacks, political votes and court cases (Williams et al 2020, p 94). That research shows the potential to renew our understanding of hate crime as a process rather than as discrete events through analysis of social media and its interrelationship with the perpetration of bias-motivated conduct offline (Williams et al 2020).

Structural inequalities are manifested in protest against DQS in the physical and psychological harm of direct violence through assault/and or intimidation as defined by criminal law, and harassment through anti-discrimination law. The diversion of resources away from inclusion and diversity initiatives such as DQS reflect the harms of indirect violence, its largely intangible impacts, and the lack of accountability of its perpetrators (Farmer 2004). The cancellation of DQS events because of security concerns raised by online and in-person threats reflects this lack of accountability (Stone 2019c). Other forms of indirect violence that channel away opportunities and resources from a particular group (Galtung 1969) in relation to DQS events can include the additional costs to secure DQS events, and the invocation of the civil law by plaintiffs in jurisdictions where they have no legal standing (see this chapter's endnotes for cases).

Networked responses to Drag Queen Storytime

The linking of protest against DQS with social media organizing by conservative Christian anti-LGBTQ+ individuals and groups (Stone 2018a, 2019c) is central to protest over DQS. This protest can include online petitions and counter petitions, and the doxing of drag performers (Stone 2019c) – through publishing their identifying information online with malicious intent and without consent – as well as the doxing of transgender performers, parents who take their children to DQS events, and anti-DQS politicians. Objections to representations of gender fluidity in reaction to DQS tap into debates over transgender identity and womanhood in the US, the UK, Australia and other Western liberal democracies.

Critics of DQS, such as high-profile Ohio-based Christian blogger and 'Activist Mommy' Elizabeth Johnston, have equated being transgender with a 'mental disorder', and public school systems that teach students about LGBTQ+ contributions to US history as 'radical leftist indoctrination centers' (Spata 2019). In the UK, aspects of gender-based criticism of DQS have included firstly, that DQS is not curriculum relevant, particularly given that early-years students do not benefit from 'men with plastic tits and spangly dresses reading books' (Bartosch 2020, np). And secondly, that DQS performances 'underscore the idea that womanhood is a gaudy, sexualised costume' (Bartosch 2020, np).

The centrality of digital media technology to performative protest that might limit rights to certain LGBTQ+ groups is exemplified in the disruption of a DQS event in Texas in June 2019 at a branch of the Austin Public Library. A representative of Infowars, a far-right conspiracy theory and fake news website, crashed the event and filmed it. The protester demanded that the drag performer disclose their non-drag name, under the auspices of transparency if someone wanted to do a background check on the performer, and which the startled performer did disclose. The performer's full name was subsequently posted with the video on Infowars, generating hundreds of comments, many of which threatened violence and employed anti-LGBTQ+ hate speech (Stone 2019c). This example also demonstrates an inverse interrelationship between offline and online amplification of bias-motivated conduct through the live streaming or filming of intimidatory behaviour at DQS events, and its subsequent amplification through posting on social media (Stone 2019c) as a form of angertainment.

This is in addition to organizing against DQS events online by the religious groups MassResistance (Laitner 2018, Stone 2019b)[4] and Warriors for Christ, who have brought civil actions against DQS events (Stone 2018b, 2019a).[5,6]

In Renton, Washington on 27 June 2019, protesters at Fairwood Library included members of the Three Percenters, many of whom were openly carrying pistols, plus members of the far-right group the Proud Boys, and the right-wing local media outlet, Operation Cold Front. According to one Three Percenter, residents opposed to DQS were worried about antifascist organizations showing up and local residents had asked the group to provide security (Stone 2019c). Upon announcement of a DQS event to be held in Olean, New York on 20 June 2019, Pennsylvania leader of the National Socialist (Nazi) Movement hate group announced plans on social media to protest the event along with others.

In addition to pre-COVID objections to DQS, are false claims posted on social media channels about the head of DQS and DQS presenters. Jaimee Michell, a founder of @gaysagainstgroomers, posted a video stating that the head of DQS was arrested on child pornography charges, which accumulated more than 17,000 likes (Funke 2022). As reported by AFP Fact Check, this fiction was based on the conflation of DQS with Brett Blomme – a former head of the Cream City LGBTQ+ Foundation, which runs a Drag Queen Story Hour programme – and who was arrested on charges of possession of child pornography. In addition to Instagram, @gaysagainstgroomers' digital ecosystem includes Twitter, Telegram, Truth Social and YouTube.

@gaysagainstgroomers is distinguished from other individuals and groups who claim that DQS is grooming children into aberrant lifestyles by claiming that it speaks for a segment of the LGBTQ+ community as 'a coalition of gays'. It sells 'gays against groomers' merchandise and its not-for-profit status is pending. In another case of misinformation, some social media users used a photograph from a DQS event in a Minneapolis suburb and reposted it, claiming that the performer exposed their genitals to children. This story was debunked by Associated Press (Swenson 2022) (for more on the representational harm of framing gay men as a threat to children, see Chapter 4).

Anti-LGBTQ+ politics and homonormativity

Outrage against DQS reveals the episodic invocation of a 'sexual emergency' (Berlant 1997). Such 'emergencies' might include prejudice-based government policies and 'defensiveness, rage, and nostalgia among ordinary citizens who liked it better when their sexuality could be assumed to be general for the population as a whole' (Berlant 1997, p 17). This protest reflects the tension between sexual citizenship as a method of achieving broader rights-bearing inclusion for LGBTQ+ communities, and the enhanced capacity to generate partisan outrage through digital media (Ellis 2023).

Bias-motivated hateful conduct against DQS readers originates in a broader politics of White grievance and related theories of 'white genocide' (Cosentino 2020). This grievance can be expressed through simplistic framing and language of 'tactical speech' that seeks to communicate directly and persuasively to a broader audience (Valverde 2010). In the context of outrage and protest against DQS, this framing perpetuates representations of gender fluidity as deviant, and a threat to children. As Russell has noted, tactical speech can erase complexity and reinforce essentialist assumptions and dominant ideas about class and respectability (Russell 2020). At the same time, this speech excludes certain LGBTQ+ groups from what Duggan (2002) has called the 'new homonormativity' of sexual politics in neoliberal discourse.

This discourse normalizes and assimilates certain kinds of sexual orientation and gender identity into mainstream culture through domesticity and consumption. For example, homonormative discourse in relation to protest against DQS can include toleration of homosexuality but can exclude the gender fluidity of drag performance; a person might not 'oppose diversity and gays', but does 'object to having transsexual [sic] individuals telling stories to "impressionable young children" at a public library' (Laitner 2018). This perspective can also intersect with 'liberal' economic arguments against the expression of gender fluidity in publicly funded premises based on inaccurate claims about expenditure of public resources on DQS events. US First Amendment freedom of speech protections and the subsequent reluctance of digital platforms to regulate speech online, in part to protect digital platform non-publisher status, and therefore limit digital platform liability (Wakabayashi 2020), have arguably amplified tactical speech online, and in person.

The disruption of a DQS event in a Brisbane, Australia, inner city library in January 2020 by members of the conservative University of Queensland Liberal National Club, mirrors elements of protest against DQS events in the US. Protesters stated that they were defending values against a corrosive gender ideology supported by ratepayer funds. Police were called to the library after it was reported that the protesters were upsetting the children there for the DQS event. However, security had moved the protesters on before police arrived (Cavanagh 2020).

Wilson Gavin, who was gay and campaigned against same-sex marriage in Australia, took his own life after a recording of the disruption of the DQS event went viral and which included Gavin at the front of the group shouting at one of the two hosts (Towle 2020). The video generated social media traffic on Twitter and Facebook with the hashtag #IStandWithQueens, while other footage from the event shows the protesters being confrontational with organizers. This incident shows the tensions and complexities of negotiating gender and sexual orientation diversity through sexual citizenship and 'homonormative' discourse, the distributive elements of this discourse,[7] the enhanced capacity to generate partisan outrage through digital media (Ellis 2023), and its potentially tragic consequences.

Domestic extremism and Western liberal 'homonationalism'

Bias-motivated reactions to DQS are caught up in a still broader, global context of the tension between the framing of Western liberal democracies as 'tolerant' and 'civilized' 'homonationalist' cultures (Puar 2007, 2013), and Christian and domestic hate and far-right groups who might challenge these claims within those cultures. Protest against DQS in Western liberal democracies is indicative of the deeper 'complexities of how "acceptance" and "tolerance" for gay and lesbian subjects have become a barometer by which the right to, and capacity for national sovereignty, is evaluated' (Puar 2013, p 336). Complicating this binary and concurrent with the advent of DQS, the political and technological context of the Trump presidency, and the broader rise of populism in the late 2010s and early 2020s, is an increased threat of domestic extremism in many Western liberal democracies.

For example, the greatest terrorism threat to US homeland security is now domestic extremists (US Department of Homeland Security 2020). In 2020, MI5 stated that violent right-wing extremism was a major threat in the UK, and that the threat of far-right plots was only second to Islamic terrorism (Sengupta 2020). In Australia, 30 per cent to 40 per cent of counter-terrorism work conducted by the Australian Security Intelligence Organisation is to combat right-wing extremism, up from approximately 10 per cent to 15 per cent prior to 2016 (Greene 2020). The starkest example of the intersection of hate rhetoric, right-wing extremism, the use of social media to amplify messages of hate, and their translation into in-person violence, are the Christchurch attacks in New Zealand in March 2019. In those attacks, an Australian self-identified member of the alt-right movement committed two consecutive terrorist attacks at mosques, killing 51 people and injuring 40 (*R* v *Tarrant* [2020] NZHC 2192), and which he live-streamed through Facebook to share with his virtual community (Tremblay 2020).

Librarians are often targeted by hate, in addition to drag presenters and the audiences assembled, with one withdrawn bill in Indiana calling for the imprisonment of librarians who distribute ill-defined 'harmful material' to minors, with six months to two and a half years in prison and up to US$10,000 in fines (Shrum 2021). More recently, in a case that exemplifies the power of framing and the unpredictability of the current digital media landscape, a benignly titled Florida bill that limits what classrooms can discuss about sexual orientation and gender identity – 'Parental Rights in Education Bill' – was reframed as the 'Don't Say Gay' bill by LGBTQ+ activists (Hesse 2022).

Conservatives responded with their own name, framing it as an 'Anti-Grooming Bill' (Hesse 2022). Christina Pushaw, press secretary for Florida Governor Ron DeSantis (Republican) tweeted, 'If you're against the Anti-Grooming Bill you are probably a groomer or at least you don't denounce the grooming of 4–8 year old children' (Hesse 2022). DeSantis went further by attacking the Walt Disney Company, after the company criticized the legislation that would severely restrict education in public schools on sexual orientation and gender identity (Shapiro 2022). Central to these attacks has been the passage of a bill by the Florida legislature, that may be overturned, to revoke Disney World's designation as a special tax district (Shapiro 2022).

At the geopolitical level, Weber (2015) has argued that the absence of a global queer theory is symptomatic of the absence of queer perspectives within international relations theory. Arguably, this absence represents an omission that does not recognize the contribution of queer theory to complex issues such as the intersection of sexuality, gender identity, procreation, religion, domestic extremism and digital technologies. An intersection manifested in in-person and online protest against DQS events noted in this chapter, and which digiqueer criminology seeks to interrogate.

Defining hateful conduct

Hate crime has been defined as crime (often violence) motivated by prejudice, bias or hatred towards a particular group of which the victim is presumed to be a member (Mason 2008). Hate crime is generally directed towards a class of people, and as such, the individual victim is often not significant to the offender and may be a stranger to them (Mason 2008). The classification of an act as a hate crime covers a broad range of offences, across a diverse range of victim groups.

In the US, a hate crime is defined by the FBI as a criminal offence with an added element of bias 'against a person or property motivated in whole or in part by an offender's bias against a race, religion, disability, sexual orientation, ethnicity, gender, or gender identity' (US Federal Bureau of Investigation nd). Hate itself is not a crime in the US and is protected under freedom of speech and other civil liberties (US Federal Bureau of Investigation n.d.). First Amendment free-speech protections in the US are in tension, for example, with the Fourteenth Amendment's implicit promise of dignity and equality (Ross 2017), and demonstrate the limits of the criminal law in addressing hate speech online that might subsequently translate into further hateful conduct in person (and the other way around). Despite this, Williams et al (2020, p 111) have found 'a consistent positive association between Twitter hate speech targeting race and religion and offline racially and religiously aggravated offences in London'.

Their study also confirmed the association between events that acted as 'triggers', such as terror attacks, political votes and court cases, for online and offline hate acts. Furthermore, they found an association in the *absence* of 'trigger' events (Williams et al 2020, emphasis added). This finding identifies the patterned nature of bias-motivated hateful conduct beyond individual incidents. The mutually constituted relationship between online and in-person hateful conduct against DQS events, and the actualization and amplification of latent, bias-motivated threats of direct and indirect violence through digital platforms, contribute further support for this claim.

In the UK, the Crown Prosecution Service uses 'hate crime' to describe a range of criminal behaviour where the perpetrator is motivated by hostility or demonstrates hostility towards a victim's 'protected characteristics' of disability, race, religion, sexual orientation or transgender identity (Crown Prosecution Service 2017). A hate crime in the UK can include verbal abuse, intimidation, threats, harassment, assault and bullying, as well as damage to property. The perpetrator can also be a friend, carer or acquaintance who exploits their relationship with the victim for financial gain or some other criminal purpose (Crown Prosecution Service 2017).

In Australia, legislation can prohibit

> public acts of vilification, [and] verbal abuse and hatred, on a range of grounds including race, religion, and sexual orientation and gender identity. Some statutes contain civil proscriptions and processes alone, while other Acts additionally establish criminal offences. The criminal proscriptions usually require an additional element – that the perpetrator has threatened, or has incited others to threaten physical harm to a person or their property. (Chapman and Kelly 2005)

However, in New South Wales in 2018, a new offence was created of 'publicly threatening or inciting violence on the grounds of race, religion, sexual orientation, gender identity or intersex or HIV/AIDS status' (Crimes Act 1900 (NSW), np), within the context in which violent reactions to DQS events have occurred.

In 2020, in response to a range of oppressive legal and police responses to LGBTIQ+ diversity in Russia and Eastern Europe, the European Commission presented its first-ever strategy on LGBTIQ+ equality in the EU. In doing so, '[t]he strategy addresses the inequalities and challenges affecting LGBTIQ+ people, setting out a number of targeted actions, including legal and funding measures' over a five-year period (European Commission 2020, np). Going further, '[t]he strategy proposes to extend the list of EU crimes to cover hate crime, including homophobic hate speech and hate crime and to bring forward the legislation on the mutual recognition of parenthood in cross-border situations' (European Commission 2020, np). Moreover, the strategy 'ensures that LGBTIQ+ concerns are well reflected in EU policy making, so that LGBTIQ people, in all their diversity, are safe and have equal opportunities to prosper and fully participate in society' (European Commission 2020, np).

Broader bias-motivated conduct in reaction to DQS events include forms of indirect violence such as threats to funding, increased oversight of decision making on public events held at public libraries, postponement or cancellation of DQS events because of threats to public safety, and/or the prohibitive cost of policing to ensure the safety of DQS events, and civil litigation. These broader strictures on LGBTQ+ expression emphasize the merit in broadening the digiqueer frame to evaluate the impact of digital media on processes of economic enfranchisement and exclusion for LGBTQ+ communities, and institutional legitimacy.

The interrelationship between sexuality, Christianity and nationalism

Bjork–James (2019) argues that a common trait of nationalist groups is to claim victimhood while advocating the right to discriminate. She further argues that religious right Christian nationalists made the 'religious value of heterosexual privilege a political mandate to shape state policy by framing Christians as the rightful determiners of state policy' (Bjork–James 2019, p 280). Bjork–James suggests that biased behaviour is a secondary effect of this moral order. The rhetorical strategy of claiming victimhood while advocating for the right to discriminate is reflected in protest against DQS. This protest can distress children through the disruption of such events, the intimidation of staff and drag presenters, and the need for an increased public and/or private security presence to safely host DQS events (Stone 2019c). Underpinning this bias is a conflation of 'Christian' and 'national' concerns based on a notion of sexual purity that pairs individual morality and national strength (Bjork–James 2019).

Bjork–James thus concludes that there is a strong relationship between sexual politics and evangelical politics in jurisdictions where there is a strong and politically organized movement that believes in a national sexuality that is integral to maintaining the moral and reproductive rights of the nation. The decoupling of Christian sexual morality from the legal institutions of the state through LGBTQ+ rights is a new form of secularism inscribed in law that threatens the privilege of such groups (Bjork-James 2019). At the same time, discriminatory politics can be rooted in a moral system and nationalist imaginary that defines others as outside the bounds of one's community (Bjork-James 2019).

Consequently, this 'moral citizenship' might accommodate bias manifested as violence. 'Sincerity' has become a common measure of such moral citizenship, particularly in the adjudication of religious freedom cases in the US 'where the sincerity of a religious subject is often measured in legal cases to determine whether or not they have experienced discrimination' (Bjork-James 2019, p 291; see also Sullivan 2018). Concurrently, the backlash against DQS reflects the amplificatory capacity and hazards of digital platforms in an era of hyper-partisanship, fuelled by the diversification of media platforms, and the polarization of political rhetoric notable in the US, the UK and Australia.

The notion of an 'androgynous mean' borne of 'the sexual revolution's reconfiguring of the human ecosystem' (Eberstadt 2019, p 28) is an additional aspect of the debate over gender identity and gender fluidity. This argument suggests that androgyny, and its instantiations of gender fluidity and gender ambiguity, operates 'as a mechanism for reconstructing the extended family/community in prosthetic form in a time when the actual Western extended family/community is in decline' (Eberstadt 2019, p 29). Ostensibly harmless DQS childhood literacy programmes are alleged to conceal the primary objective of indoctrinating and recruiting children into the alleged aberrant drag lifestyle because drag queens cannot 'reproduce' (Stone 2019c). This argument frames the gender fluidity debate as a tension between traditional notions of family predicated on the procreative contract between married men and women, and the tribalism of broader gender identity politics harnessed through digital media.

This apocalyptic vision of procreative decline conflates gender fluidity with a reproductive scarcity that endangers

Western civilization. This is despite access to in-vitro fertilization, and the extension of adoption and marriage rights to same-sex attracted people in some Western liberal jurisdictions. Conservative Christian anti-LGBTQ+ hate group activism, and far-right anti-LGBTQ+ reactions to DQS in the US, are tied up in deeper debates of White grievance interconnected with such notions of cultural primacy. Fringe spaces on the internet, such as 4chan, 8chan and Reddit, have been integral in accommodating this grievance, and its translation into a growing wave of violent actions by White nationalists worldwide (Cosentino 2020) (see 2019, El Paso, Texas shooting; 2019 Halle, Germany synagogue shooting, streamed through Twitch; and 2019 Poway, San Diego, synagogue shooting). These actions are part of a victimization narrative perpetrated by people of White ethnicity under the auspices of the 'Great Replacement' conspiracy theory (Cosentino 2020). This conspiracy theory, and related theories of 'white genocide', claim that the genetic and cultural heritage of White people, in the US and other countries, are under threat by means of miscegenation and forced assimilation with non-White immigrants (Cosentino 2020).

Co-option of DQS by religious and political conservatives as reflective of the degeneracy of conventional 'liberalism', is another aspect of protest against DQS (Wallace-Wells 2019). Political debates about 'liberalism' and nationhood have been charged by an incivility deemed necessary by some conservatives to regain the political and moral ground allegedly lost by conservatives since the late 1960s, particularly in the US (Wallace-Wells 2019). The broader implication of claims from conservatives who reject the right to express divergent viewpoints is that they seemingly advocate a revision of norms of freedom of expression based on 'higher good' rhetoric that excludes divergent viewpoints (Wallace-Wells 2019), and the normalization of exclusion through information warfare.

Conversely, drag queens reading to children in public libraries can be seen as reflective of the domestication of the 'cultural left', whose mainstream rights focus for LGBT people has for some time been the family-friendly focus of marriage and children, not sexual liberation (Goldberg 2019). This perspective reflects the homonormalization of marriage and procreation for same-sex attracted people through sexual citizenship discourse. The deeper political significance of conservative reactions to DQS in the US is its embodiment of the fracturing of the 'fusionist' coalition of the modern right, which had long united social conservatives, economic libertarians and foreign policy hawks (Goldberg 2019).

'Deceptive' bodies and Drag Queen Storytime as a site of hyper-partisanship

Demonizing rhetoric grounded in harmful pseudoscience that portrays LGBTQ+ people as threats to children, society and public health are central themes of anti-LGBTQ+ organizing, and ideology in opposition to LGBTQ+ rights, including the organizing of anti-LGBTQ+ hate groups (Southern Poverty Law Center 2020a). Goldberg (2019) has noted that the perceived risks of DQS to childhood meaning-making of identity are somewhat skewed in a political environment that has seen the rise of right-wing extremism in the US.

Protests of DQS by right-wing extremists who incite violence online and then may translate this violence into in-person bias-motivated hateful conduct, and the other way around, demonstrates that the legacy of legal and medical stigma of same-sex attraction and gender fluidity based on claims of their harmfulness to children is close to the surface. That this conduct might be carried out in public institutions such as libraries, in some instances by armed protesters, and to the visible distress of children, reflects elements of Bjork-James' (2019) argument about the exclusivity of perceived moral citizenship based on national identity. The ease with which these sentiments can be amplified through social media speak to Williams et al's (2020) identification of a more general pattern of correlation between online hate speech targeting race and religion and offline racially and religiously aggravated crimes independent of 'trigger' events. As noted earlier, broader justifications of hateful conduct against drag queens reading to children in public spaces are predicated on the age inappropriateness of 'adult' drag queen performers reading to children, and alleged use of public resources to cater to the 'corruption' of childhood innocence (Stone 2019c).

To varying degrees, and dependant on jurisdiction, the themes discussed in this chapter emphasize the recursive conflation of gender fluidity, same-sex attraction, and transgender identity with deviance to justify hateful conduct. Negative reactions to DQS reflect the intersection of expression rights that recognize LGBTQ+ inclusion and diversity through sexual citizenship discourse, and moral objections to expression of these rights based on arguments of sexual purity that eschew gender fluidity.

Underscoring hyper-partisan political debate over DQS are objections to gender fluidity that originate in the criminal law preoccupation with categorizing bodies as procreative binaries rather than, as Brooks and Thompson (2019) have argued, reaching a judgement as to the ethical balance, for example, in determining consent in cases that involve gender fluidity. This categorization through the criminal law might perpetuate stigmatization of gender fluidity through the framing of gender-fluid bodies as 'deceptive', 'gender deviant', or bodies to be 'feared' (Brooks and Thompson 2019). Some DQS protesters extrapolate the 'deceptive' framing of gender fluidity of drag performance to paedophilia, a label that perpetuates the imaginary of same-sex attraction and gender fluidity as deviant and a threat to children.

Claims of religious, moral and cultural superiority in the face of the failure of religious institutions to protect children against institutional child sex abuse (Commonwealth of Australia 2017, Laitner 2018) speak to the durability of faith-based tactical speech that can perpetuate systemic representational harms against vulnerable populations. The doxing of a drag performer in Austin, Texas noted earlier (Stone 2019c), taps into the notion of gender fluidity as deceptive. At the same time, the use of doxing against transgender performers, parents who take their children to DQS events, and anti-DQS politicians, reflects the pernicious and pervasive nature of doxing as a structured, technological harm, and a hate tactic used across the political spectrum.

Information warfare, social media and the hate feedback loop

The ongoing importance of recognition for LGBTQ+ rights is grounded in the failure of criminal justice institutions to invoke criminal law in Western liberal democracies in the second half of the 20th century in response to claims of discrimination by minority groups (Mason 2014). This included extreme violence against groups such as African Americans, Roma, and gays and lesbians. This failure has perpetuated the criminalization, pathologization and stigmatization of LGBTQ+ communities and others, and which engendered the hate crime movement that invoked identity politics as an organizing strategy (Mason 2014).

At the same time, the establishment of a legitimate media frame for LGBTQ+ sexual citizenship discourse in Western liberal democracies through the identity politics movement has developed a reasonable capacity for some of those communities to resist ongoing and new forms of marginalization through social and political organizing. However, the ongoing necessity to resource campaigns to secure basic relationship rights for communities whose political status cannot be taken for granted, such as LGBTQ+ communities, and for freedom from state interference in jurisdictions where same-sex conduct is still criminalized and pathologized, further exemplifies the channelling away of resources from such communities. This contrasts with rights-bearing citizens who do not need to secure or defend such basic rights through political campaigning.

The translation of threats online to threats in person, and the other way around, and the translation of discriminatory beliefs into discriminatory policy in a 'feedback loop' (Bjork-James 2019), speak to the interrelationship between direct and indirect violence and the perpetuation of structural violence – present when somatic and mental realizations are below their potential (Galtung 1969, p 167) – against LGBTQ+ people through digital media technologies, in person and through civil litigation. This can invoke the 'hate feedback loop' through networked protest, the amplification of that protest through social media, and its subsequent oscillation between traditional news media and social media, and in-person protest (Ellis 2021, 2023). This feedback loop is suggestive of Williams et al's (2020) identification of a more general pattern of correlation between online hate speech targeting race and religion and offline racially and religiously aggravated crimes independent of 'trigger' events.

A political and media climate of permissiveness of hateful conduct, particularly up until mid-2020 (Hern 2020, Roose 2020), is arguably a form of structural violence that has manifested in actual violence. However, and while acknowledging that some digital platforms have made their policies on hateful conduct more explicit (Roose 2020), the digital platforms that have the largest reach in English are US-owned, and therefore their broad policy parameters on hateful conduct have been developed mindful of US freedom of speech protections and their non-publisher status (Mason and Czapski 2017).

The range of criminal, civil and distributive protest against DQS noted in this chapter are continuations of the constraint of structural violence through digital media that allow for inter-jurisdictional networked protest, and which represents the reinterpretation and application of structural violence over time (Farmer 2004).

This catalogue of legal, medical and economic proscription is in spite of the progress made in jurisdictions to decriminalize same-sex conduct, to expunge historical same-sex offences, enact marriage equality, and legislate against conversion therapies (ILGA World 2020a). Overall, this data emphasizes the variability in, and political expediency of, rights enfranchisement in communities whose political status cannot be taken for granted (Loader and Sparks 2013).

Conclusion

This chapter has analysed the interplay between online bias-motivated hateful conduct, its translation into in-person bias-motivated conduct, and the other way around. The politicization of DQS, and this amplification of bias-motivated conduct through digital media technologies, represents the reinterpretation and application of structural violence over time. The patterned nature of some of this conduct shows the limitations of criminal law in addressing such conduct as discrete incidents. Discriminatory beliefs can translate into discriminatory policy, perpetuating direct and indirect violence against LGBTQ+ communities and episodic amplification of the hate feedback loop. These discriminatory beliefs are grounded in Christian righteousness that has made a religious value of heterosexual privilege, and a political mandate to shape state policy by framing Christians as the rightful determiners of state policy. These claims can be co-opted by Christian conservative politicians and commentators, anti-LGBTQ+ hate groups, and far-right groups, to justify the perpetuation of direct and indirect violence against LGBTQ+ individuals and communities. That these harms are perpetuated in jurisdictions such as the US, the UK, and Australia, where same-sex marriage is lawful, and conduct rights have been expanded over decades for LGBTQ+ peoples, shows the necessity for ongoing research into representational harms. The resilience of DQS in the face of the spectrum of harms the integration of the social and the digital represent to LGBTQ+ communities, speaks to the resilience of those communities through social and political organizing, and the necessity to remain vigilant.

FOUR

(Mis)Representation of Same-Sex Attraction

Introduction

As noted in earlier chapters, representational harms against same-sex conduct and related gender diversity can drive ongoing stigma against LGBTQ+ peoples that reinforces inequity (Colbran 2022). This can include misrecognition, erasure, omission, or covert surveillance of LGBTQ+ identity. Moreover, gender non-conformity is often conflated with homosexuality, and as such, same-sex attraction is a catalyst for anti-LGBTQ+ hate, and organized responses to that hate (Duncan et al 2019).

This chapter analyses the relationship between digital knowledge production processes, misrecognition of same-sex attraction and homophobia, and the broadening of LGBTQ+ cultural representation in popular culture and advertising as a strategy to minimize representational harms. The chapter also considers the impact of ongoing masculine gender role enforcement on the negotiation of same-sex attraction within the broader social environment, and within same-sex relations. The sharper focus on same-sex attraction in this chapter is based on the prevalence of legal, political and social proscription against same-sex conduct, and political organizing around same-sex expression, conduct and relationship rights (OutRight Action International 2018, ILGA World 2020a, 2020b).

This chapter first summarizes the range of stigma against same-sex attraction, with a focus on representational harms perpetrated by or through digital platforms. Then discussed is the impact of continued same-sex attracted stigma on a range of same-sex attracted groups, and the role that gender role enforcement might play in reasoning behind this continued stigma. It then applies the human capabilities approach to LGBT inclusion and economic development as an additional avenue through which to secure LGBTQ+ enfranchisement, and in doing so integrates research on same-sex attraction and the market (Richardson 2018).

The chapter suggests that macroeconomic approaches to identifying the intrinsic value of individuals based on their capacity, rather than on their sexual expression, conduct or relationships, might mitigate representational harms. At the same time, the chapter considers that this approach can perpetuate medico-legal categorizations based on sexual conduct rather than identity, and notions of homonormativity. However, if the final destination is autonomy, as Galtung (1969) and others argue (Solanke 2017), then prioritizing agency through macroeconomic data presents another lever through which to address the inequalities of structural violence amplified by representational harms through hybrid media, and as noted in Chapter 3. The literature drawn on is based on a combination of keyword searches: 'representational harms', 'same sex attraction', 'heteronormativity' and 'violence against same sex attraction'. The chapter argues that increasing consideration of same-sex attraction as identity rather than conduct has generated increased LGBTQ+ representation through streaming and social narrative videos by major corporations to increase positive representations of LGBTQ+ identification (Nielsen 2021). A recent campaign by Gillette is used as a case study. Yet amid this context, is also an increase in anti-LGBTQ+ hate.

Context and consequences of stigma against same-sex attraction

Central to the reinforcement of stigmatization or erasure of diverse sexual expression through representational harms is Foucault's articulation of the confluence of power and knowledge in discourse, its instability, and its capacity to produce meaning (Foucault, 1981, p 71). The identification of the homosexual as a 'species', and the criminalization and psychiatrization of its 'perversions', thus rendered the notion of same-sex attraction as inherent to that 'species', rather than its potential across the general population. As such, the homosexual comes into being not as 'some natural property inherent in sex itself, but by virtue of the tactics of power immanent in' discourse (Foucault, 1981, p 70).

The hierarchical categorization of homosexuality through the sexological medical models of modernity have more recently been documented and analysed by Weeks (2017). Subsequent historical studies of the West and cross-cultural studies illustrate that Foucault's basic insight is accurate; notable in research on male sexual behaviours and AIDS/HIV that has established that many men who have sex with men (MSM) do not identify as 'gay' (Youde 2019), 'breaking the essentialist link between sexuality and identity' (Richardson and Robinson 2020, p 85).

Criminological research has enumerated the indicative prevalence of physical violence against same-sex attraction, and the extreme nature of that violence, and the invocation of 'homosexual advance defences' as an extended form of discrimination, long after the decriminalization of homosexuality in some jurisdictions (Mason and Tomsen 1997, Mouzos and Thompson 2000, Tomsen 2002, Robinson 2008, Callaghan et al 2018, Ellis 2021). Less has been written about the impact of, and reasoning behind ongoing representational harms against same-sex attraction, and its relationship to heteronormativity and homophobia (van der Toorn et al 2020).

Enumerating representational harms against same-sex attraction is significant given that '[d]epicting gay men as a threat to children may be the single most potent weapon for stoking public fears about homosexuality – and for winning elections and referenda' in the US (Southern Poverty Law Center 2011, np), and related framing through media in

Australia and other jurisdictions. Underscoring this context are the intact social origins of stigma despite the decriminalization of same-sex conduct in a growing number of jurisdictions, the expansion of legitimate categories of vulnerability enshrined in anti-discrimination law (Solanke 2017), and progress made on marriage equality.

As noted in Chapter 1, in clarifying the purpose of anti-discrimination law, Solanke shows that it is the social meaning applied to an attribute that is the driver of stigma, not the attribute itself (Solanke 2017, p 29). As such, cultural and political context, and digital platform architecture, inform the consequences of LGBTQ+ performances of identity to digital audiences (Robards et al 2021).

Episodic amplification of representational harms based on legacy pseudo-scientific, legal and medical same-sex pathologies, and religious beliefs that might underpin them, show the social embeddedness of stigma against same-sex attraction. This embeddedness is demonstrated in why researchers in 2018 would even bother trying to develop an algorithm to determine a person's same-sex attraction through facial recognition software (Wang and Kosinski 2018). But also why this capacity might be of interest to marketers, or law enforcers, particularly in jurisdictions where same-sex conduct is criminalized. Or why a traditional news media outlet in 2022 might still coerce a celebrity to come out, despite the newsworthiness of celebrity status outside same-sex attraction, as was the case with actor Rebel Wilson. It was perhaps unsurprising that Wilson came out on Instagram, but at the same time is indicative of the contradictions of social media platforms given the representational harms facilitated against LGBTQ+ expression on those platforms noted throughout this book.

Representational harms as a frame can incorporate how legislatures can generate 'debate-related stress' over relationship rights, such as the same-sex marriage postal survey in Australia in 2017, that 'represented an acute external minority stress event that had measurable negative impacts on mental health of LGBTIQ people and their allies' (Ecker et al 2019, p 285). As did the legislative process in Ireland over the marriage equality debate there (Verrelli et al 2019, p 336). Misrepresentation might explain why qualitative research (n=100) analysing reasons for de-transitioning found that 23 out of 100 respondents expressed homophobia or difficulty accepting oneself as lesbian, gay or bisexual as a reason for transition, and subsequent detransition (Littman 2021). Moreover, that access to positive representations of same-sex attraction could assist to align one's internal identity with external signifiers (Littman 2021). Or why, in Russia, '[i]n addition to the efforts to criminalize speech, Russian government authorities with the Investigative Committee, a federal anti-corruption oversight body, had planned to arrest gay fathers in Russia under child trafficking laws and "allegedly [threatened] to place their children in foster care for the duration of the investigation"' (Insikt Group 2021, p 7).

In the UK, both women and men experience online harassment. However, women and the LGBTQ+ population are more likely to experience a wider variety of online abuse, including more serious doxing-related violations, and being the targets of revenge porn and nude leaked messages (Access Now 2021). The harms of outing continue online, and can result in the loss of homes and jobs (House of Lords and House of Commons 2021). In a recent case in Western Australia, the gamification of outing on TikTok through the 'Guess Who' trend resulted in the resignation of a gay teacher from a Catholic school (Roberts 2022). According to the Australian inquiry into online safety, women who identify as LGBTIQA+ were more likely to experience online abuse than women in general (Commonwealth of Australia 2022). This is within the broader context of people who identify as LGBTIQA+ or gender-divergent at a higher risk of online harm (Commonwealth of Australia 2022).

'Shadowbanning' – blocking a user from a social media site or online forum without their knowledge, typically by making their posts and comments no longer visible to other users – has discriminated against LGBTQ+ people, people of colour and people with disabilities (Salty 2019, Rauchberg 2022). Moderation guidelines from TikTok for jurisdictions where same-sex conduct is unlawful have resulted in the underrepresentation of diverse LGBTQ+ identification through banning of any content that could be seen as positive to gay people or gay rights, down to same-sex couples holding hands, even in countries where that conduct is lawful (Hern 2019).

Such is the extent of the malicious targeting of 'groomers' – a term used to spread unfounded accusations of child abuse against LGBTQ+ people – through handles such as Libs of TikTok and @gaysagainstgroomers on Instagram, that Twitter announced a ban in July 2022 on targeted use of the term (Gingerich 2022). 'Hate raids' on social media platform Twitch (and others) have targeted diverse LGBTQ+ expression through bot-powered accounts that 'spew racist, sexist, and homophobic language and content' (*Twitch Interactive Inc* v *CruzzControl, CreatineOverdose* [2021, p 2]). Lateral violence and abuse online (eSafety Commissioner 2021, Tran et al 2022) can be enacted from within the LGBTQ+ community on other members (eSafety Commissioner 2021), misogyny in particular (Hale and Ojeda 2018).

In the Middle East, members of the LGBTQ+ community have limited freedoms and protections against discrimination and have endured online attacks, surveillance and censorship (Insikt Group 2020). In many countries, governments have used domestic telecommunications companies to block pro-LGBTQIA+ apps and websites. Further, law enforcement have deployed the use of entrapment to expose members of the LGBTQIA+ community for imprisonment and torture (Insikt Group 2020). Similar activity was observed affecting LGBTQIA+ individuals in various Asian countries in recent years, specifically Azerbaijan, China, Georgia, India, Indonesia, Malaysia, Myanmar, Pakistan, Singapore, South Korea and Sri Lanka. Many of these attacks were instigated by the state for censorship or surveillance purposes, or by individual actors motivated by financial interests or social stigma (Insikt Group 2020). Networked hate against Malaysian transgender public figure Nur Sajat Kamaruzzaman has seen her flee to Australia (Tatum 2022).

The lingering social stigma towards the LGBTQIA+ community and the growing influence of evangelical Christian groups in Brazil and Central America pose the greatest threats to LGBTQIA+ rights in Latin America. Across much of Africa, the LGBTQIA+ community is perceived, and framed, as a threat to society that states' are combatting through organized crackdowns, surveillance and censorship. In some instances, African governments are partnering with private sector surveillance organizations to target 'high risk' groups, which includes the LGBTQIA+ community. Entrapment by law enforcement agencies and criminals is a common theme of coercion observed across Africa, with the outing of LGBTQIA+ individuals posing a significant threat due to strict anti-LGBTQIA+ legislation and socially conservative views among the public (Insikt Group 2020).

A renewed emphasis on binary gender conformity in China has allegedly increased censorship of LGBT student messaging apps, among others (Gan and Xiong 2021). Stigmatization of same-sex attraction in Russia through anti-LGBTQ+ propaganda legislation can include targeted cyberattacks, censorship, and surveillance (Insikt Group 2020), while surveillance and censorship has been documented as widespread across Russia and Eastern Europe (Insikt Group 2020). Russian anti-LGBTQ+ disinformation through messaging apps and digital platforms such as Telegram, while mainly directed at Russian users (Insikt Group 2022), speak to the pervasiveness of Russian 'traditional values' rhetoric that is readily endorsed by 'manosphere' groups elsewhere (Nicholas and Agius 2018), notably armed right-wing groups in the US. This creation of a common enemy, and coercion of LGBTQ+ people, shows how regimes distract from political mismanagement through the imaginary of same-sex attraction and sexual and gender diversity as aberrant.

Sexual orientation, gender identity or gender expression change efforts (SOGIECE) (otherwise known as 'conversion therapy' or 'ex-gay therapy') include interventions such as 'electroshock aversion therapy', 'chemical aversion therapy', 'internment in clinics or camps' and 'exorcism and spiritual/ miracle cures' (ILGA World 2020a). Algorithms on social media platforms can lead users down a 'rabbit hole' once they find a 'conversion therapy' provider (Global Project Against Hate and Extremism 2022a). Almost all searches for 'reintegrative therapy' and 'unwanted same-sex attraction' return unauthoritative material (Global Project Against Hate and Extremism 2022a). Less moderation in non-English speaking jurisdictions means that anti-LGBTQ+ bigotry can go unchecked in those jurisdictions (Global Project Against Hate and Extremism 2022a), often in places that criminalize same-sex conduct.

Bans on conversion therapy in some US jurisdictions have been generally successful in protecting minors (Wuest 2021). However, the revanchist movement continues to seek and legitimize fringe views (Wuest 2021). Insikt Cyber Threat Analysis rightly notes that criminalizing stigma against LGBTQIA+ peoples will continue to encourage criminal acts against those peoples (Insikt Group 2020), and justify continued targeting, surveillance and censorship through the framing of LGBTQIA+ individuals and communities as an external threat to security, society or morality (Insikt Group 2020).

Homophobia, the homosocial and gender identity stress

A starting point in integrating sexual identity negotiation, its relationship with (mis)recognition, and the capacity of that recognition to address inequity through market forces is to identify the origins of violence against same-sex attraction and the structures that can exacerbate or ameliorate it. Altman (1971/2012) in particular has argued that the violence and sexual exploitation of patriarchal heteronormative masculinity stigmatized gay men because they subverted the solidarity of the patriarchy. Sedgwick has argued that heterosexual masculinity has been defined and structured around the violent exclusion of homosexual male desire. She contrasts this exclusion with the inclusiveness of 'homosocial' desire manifested in men helping men maintain economic, social and cultural privileges, and which she argues is in contrast to the inherently feminine and anti-masculine framing of 'gayness' (Sedgwick 1985).

Sedgwick claims that homophobia serves to demarcate the boundaries between the economic underpinnings of the homosocial, and the physical desire of the homosexual, a demarcation that is 'essentially anti-feminist as it depends on women as currency in which homosocial male-to-male interactions can continue without being regarded, framed or understood as homosexual' (Nebeling Petersen and Hvidtfeldt 2020, p 9). As such, masculinity can be 'conceptualized as hierarchical power relations to the feminine and to other forms of masculinity, and thus, masculinity is constructed and enabled by homophobia and the escape from the feminine' (Nebeling Petersen and Hvidtfeldt 2020, p 9).

Research on gender role enforcement can shed light on aspects of the relationship between traditional forms of masculinity and the durability of stigma against male same-sex attraction in particular. One study that used stimulus of same-sex male intimacy has found that adherence to the antifemininity norm exerted an indirect effect, primarily through sexual prejudice, on increases in anger toward the gay, but not the heterosexual, male (Parrott 2009). An online study of 978 men who were shown a video clip depicting male–male intimacy found that authoritarian and traditionally masculine men respond to depictions of male–male intimacy with anger, that this anger predicts greater aggression against a gay male target than a heterosexual target, but that anonymity did not influence the link between anger and aggression (Goodnight 2016).

Linkages can be made between masculine gender role stress and the relationship between the (mis)recognition of same-sex attraction in conjunction with 'research that examines the deeply entwined contexts and elements that undergird networked misogyny' (Banet-Weiser and Miltner 2016, p 173). For example, the relationship between homophobia and entrenchment of the homosocial and its engagement in networked misogyny can be found in online manosphere forums through homophobic comments that are used 'to insult those who are perceived to be non-masculine' (Jones et al 2020, p 1910). For example, that male feminists are 'gay' (Jones et al 2020), and that a man is weak because of the 'dick up their arse' (Jones et al 2020, p 1910).

Negative reactions to co-option of social movements by consumer-focused brands, such as Gillette's 'The Best Men Can Be' campaign (discussed in detail below), show the continued intersectional significance of networked misogyny, stigma against same-sex attraction, and manosphere responses to challenges to conventional masculinity (Trott 2020), manifested in product boycotts, and armed protest against the gender fluidity of drag performance at DQS childhood literacy events. They may also shed light on reasoning behind internalized homophobia (Thepsourinthone et al 2020), the impact of social media on body image perceptions and bodily practices among gay, bisexual, and other men who have sex with men (Filice et al 2020), and the origins of violence against same-sex attracted men (Baugher and J.A. Gazmararian 2015).

Taken together,

theory pertaining to the precarious or fragile state of masculinity would suggest that men who are anxious about adapting to shifting standards of masculinity may experience deep fear about living up to changing masculine norms, which increases potential for men to become confused, reactive, and aggressive when perceptions of gender norms shift. (Bogen et al 2021, p 102)

Hale and Ojeda (2018) provide broader context on the relationship between misrepresentation and imprecise definitions of concepts that impede the recognition of discrimination. They argue that the under-theorizing of misogyny beyond description contributes to the ongoing slipperiness of misogyny as a concept and one that 'provides a smokescreen, giving it additional cause to go unnoticed or complexifying criticism of it' (Hale and Ojeda 2018, p 311). Hale and Ojeda argue that this slipperiness can leave gay male misogyny unrecognized because of its sexually marginalized status (Hale and Ojeda 2018). They use the concept of 'effemminophobia' to articulate this argued manifestation of misogyny, and its regulatory power within LGBTQ+ communities and society at large (Hale and Ojeda 2018).

Enduring stigma against same-sex attraction may be the motivation for gender transition that does not reconcile that attraction. In research on detransition, 'some de-transitioners return to identifying with their birth sex, some assume (or maintain) a nonbinary identification, and some continue to identify as transgender' (Littman 2021, p 3367). More detailed findings from that research show that '[t]he internalized homophobia/difficulty accepting oneself as a lesbian female, gay male, or bisexual person narrative (n=23/100) consisted of descriptions that the respondents' discomfort and distress about being lesbian, gay, or bisexual was related to their gender dysphoria, transition, or detransition, or that they assumed they were transgender because they did not yet understand themselves to be lesbian, gay or bisexual. All of the participants in that 'category indicated that they were either same-sex attracted exclusively or were same-sex attracted in combination with opposite-sex attraction (such as bisexual, pansexual, etc.)' (Littman 2021, p 3362). The researchers did not assume that homophobia was a reason for detransitioning and the following responses were written in as 'other' for the question about why participants transitioned: '[t]ransitioning to male would mean my attraction to girls would be "normal"'; 'being a "gay trans man" (female dating other females) felt better than being a lesbian, less shameful'; 'I felt being the opposite gender would make my repressed same-sex attraction less scary'; 'I didn't want to be a gay man' (Littman 2021, p 3363).

These responses provide insight into the mutually constituted relationship between representational harms against same-sex attraction and the rejection of related identities from participants who noted that it took time for them to gain an understanding of themselves as lesbian, gay or bisexual, reflected in the following comments: "At the time I was trying to figure out my identity and felt very male and thought I was transgender. I later discovered that I was a lesbian"; and "Well, after deep discovery, I realized I was a gay man and realized that a sexual trauma after puberty might [have] confused my thought. I wanted to live as a gay man again" (Littman 2021, p 3363).

In terms of the value of the visibility of diverse LGBTQ+ sexualities, '[s]everal natal female respondents expressed that seeing other butch lesbians would have been helpful to them as shown by the following: "What would have helped me is being able to access women's community, specifically lesbian community. I needed access to diverse female role-models and mentors, especially other butch women"' (Littman 2021, p 3363). The researchers concluded that '[c]ontinued work is needed to reduce rigid gender roles, increase representation of gender stereotype nonconformity, and to address discrimination and social pressures exerted against people who are transgender, lesbian, gay, bisexual, and gender stereotype non-conforming' (Littman 2021, p 3367).

Masculinity and male same-sex harassment and assault

The underreporting and under-identification of male-to-male sexual assault (Bullock and Beckson 2011, Kiss et al 2020) demonstrates the durability of stigma associated with same-sex attraction and how this might inhibit a victim-survivor's capacity or willingness to disclose. Inherent in that unwillingness is the shame associated with a man's inability to ward off unwanted sexual attention from a man because of notions of masculinity ascribed to the 'powerful male body'. For example, US actor Terry Crews noted the masculine stereotypes he faced when he disclosed that he had been sexually harassed by a male entertainment executive. It is notable in that case that it was scepticism about female victim-survivor disclosure of sexual violence that prompted Crews to disclose his own experience of sexual harassment (Bradley 2018). Crews has stated that male accusers can benefit, and be hurt by pre-existing notions about masculinity (Bradley 2018); some people seemed quicker to believe his claims because he is a man, but some sceptics also blamed Crews for misconstruing the intentions of his harasser, or wondered why Crews did not object through physical violence, while ignoring the consequences Crews could have faced in doing so (Bradley 2018).

Crews' case and others (Bradley 2018) raise this topical issue of the extent to which sexual assault of men and boys is downplayed because of the stigma of same-sex attraction and of male rape. This stigma can complicate trauma for male victim-survivors of sexual violence. Among the reasons why male sexual assault victim-survivors have been excluded from consideration of victimhood is that male victims are perceived as more likely to be homosexual, and that as such they are perceived as actually wanting the assault (Duncanson 2013). At the same time, research into the prevalence of sexual violence in same-sex relationships shows comparable or higher interpartner violence among lesbian and gay couples than among heterosexual couples (Rollè et al 2018). Further misconceptions are that men in the civilian community simply cannot be victims of sexual assault; that the incidence of sexual assault of males is so rare as not to merit attention; and that male victims are more responsible for their assault than female victims.

Stigma against same-sex attraction is found in reluctance of US male college students to report sexual assault for concern that they would be judged as gay (Sable et al 2006), and in cases of 'brooming' as a hazing ritual, where the victim-survivor might be quizzed about whether the perpetrators were gay (Brown 2021). The stigma is also perpetrated by international tribunals such as the International Criminal Court, who recently refused to hear a case about male rape in Uganda, while regularly holding hearings with women and girls over allegations of rape (*The Prosecutor* v *Dominic Ongwen* [2021] ICC-02/04-01/15). The need for dedicated support services for male victim-survivors of sexual violence is in part an acknowledgement of the internalization of stigma related to same-sex male rape (Kiss et al 2020). These misconceptions can be amplified by commentators in the knowledge that stigma will prevent many same-sex attracted victim-survivors from coming forward, and which allows ongoing misrecognition that can justify misrepresentation of same-sex conduct in certain contexts.

The human capabilities approach to addressing same-sex representational harms

The litany of stigma against same-sex attraction noted above, even in 'liberal' jurisdictions, suggests that there is some way to go to maximize the benefit of same-sex attraction as identity, rather than conduct. To make the relationship between sexuality and the market explicit, Badgett et al (2019) have enumerated LGBT syndemic vulnerability – 'a predisposition to the development of clustering and interacting diseases or health conditions that results from shared exposure to a set of adverse social conditions' (Slagboom et al 2020, p 7) – in relation to violence, workplace discrimination and education to make the case for the mutual reinforcement of LGBT inclusion and economic development underscored by the four principles of the capabilities approach:

1. **Human capital and economic potential** – that greater inclusion of LGBT people could expand an economy's human capital by generating opportunities for LGBT people to enhance their human capital through more education, better health outcomes or additional job-related training.
2. **Post-materialist demand for human rights** – that countries are more likely to value minority rights after they have developed economically and become more economically secure (Inglehart 1981, 2008).
3. **Strategic modernization** – links LGBT inclusion and the economy through a country's interest in strategies that enhance both inclusion and economic development and reflect a country's modernization and openness (Weiss 2007).
4. **Achievement of capabilities** – 'the capabilities approach conceptualizes development as an expansion of freedom for individuals to make choices about what they can do and be, with that expansion not dependent upon individuals' membership in certain identity groups' (Badgett et al 2019, p 4; see also Nussbaum 2001, Sen 1999).

Increased positive representation of diverse LGBTQ+ identification across a range of media support this claim. However, as noted through many of the examples in this book, even in jurisdictions such as the US where major tech companies might support the four planks of the human capabilities approach described here, they also continue to platform those who seek to undermine it.

As noted earlier, Badgett et al have challenged the assumption of universal LGBTQ+ syndemic vulnerability by segmenting LGBTQ+ demographics. Badgett has also documented the discriminatory tax burden that same-sex couples might pay, showing in 2007 that same-sex couples paid on average more than US$1,000 annually than similarly situated opposite-sex couples whose marriage is recognized (Santoscoy

2012). Some companies and institutions have altered their employee compensation and benefits to remedy the disparity (Santoscoy 2012).

The representational harms against same-sex attraction in advertising have shifted in recent years in some Western liberal democracies to recognition in varied ways. The post-materialist values argument finds resonance here, too.

In a meta-analysis, Eisen and Hermann (2019) empirically assessed the net persuasive effects of homosexual versus heterosexual imagery in advertising, and of gay versus lesbian imagery in advertising. Their purpose was to uncover the conditions under which either or both imageries lead to more persuasion and benefit in advertising effectiveness (Eisend and Hermann 2019, p 381). They identify that incongruence between factors of imagery, consumer characteristics, cultural values, explicitness of imagery, endorser gender, and product type results in unfavourable responses to homosexual advertising imagery (Eisend and Hermann 2019). They argue that societies with high levels of wealth and education develop a higher level of social trust, and therefore are more receptive to depictions of homosexual intimacy within the parameters of the factors outlined above. This finding correlates with Badgett et al's (2019) point on post-materialist demands for human rights, such as political freedom and participation, self-actualization, personal relationships and creativity.

Concurrently, '[d]iversity in advertising portrayals can prime most consumers to think about others, which leads to perceived social connectedness, empathy, and the appreciation of diversity in advertising imagery' (Eisend and Hermann 2019, p 395; see also Akestam et al 2017). Eisend and Hermann (2019, p 395) found that homosexual consumers 'are more persuaded by homosexual than heterosexual portrayals'. And that homosexual consumers react negatively toward heterosexual imagery. This is an inverse finding from prior research that suggested that heterosexual consumers react negatively to homosexual imagery (Eisend and Hermann

2019, p 395). 'Lesbian endorsers are preferred over gay male endorsers by heterosexual consumers, in line with suggestions by Oakenfull and Greenlee (2004), who recommend using lesbian endorsers as they lead to more positive responses by heterosexual consumers' (Eisend and Hermann 2019, p 395).

More recently, the recognition of the value of the 'rainbow family' as a market segment has generated more recognition through greater screen presence and the quality of that screen presence (Nielsen 2021), and to distributive effects through tolerance and acceptance. The growth in LGBTQ+ representation in advertising, and the quality of that advertising, demonstrates the benefits of broader approaches in addressing representational harms against queer identities beyond sexuality.

At the same time, the collective buying power of LGBTQ peoples in the US was estimated to be nearly US$1 trillion in 2017, rivalling the disposable income of all other American minority groups (Chesney 2017). Another avenue of potential revenue loss or gain is that LGBTQ allies would support LGBTQ people in advertising, and may support protest against anti-LGBTQ media. Recent research about LGBTQ inclusion in advertising and media has found that most non-LGBTQ people personally know at least one LGBTQ person in their own lives, a higher level than ever before; non-LGBTQ people are very comfortable with LGBTQ people appearing in the TV, movies and ads they consume, opening the door for more opportunities in the future; non-LGBTQ people who are exposed to LGBTQ media images are more likely to experience increasing levels of acceptance and comfort towards LGBTQ people; and companies benefit from including LGBTQ people in advertisements, with the vast majority of non-LGBTQ consumers looking favourably on companies that do so (GLAAD and Procter and Gamble 2019).

Strategic modernization resonates with Puar's conceptualization of 'homonationalism', within which (some) homosexual bodies have been deemed worthy of recognition (and protection) by nation states, redefining 'the relationship between the state, capitalism, and sexuality' (Puar 2013, p 336). So while the 'complexities of how "acceptance" and "tolerance" for gay and lesbian subjects have become a barometer by which the right to, and capacity for national sovereignty is evaluated' (Puar 2013, p 336), how and when states use those levers is indicative of their commitment to those causes and how they can be used politically. Within an unstable geopolitical environment, a focus on economics can contribute to continued widening of the context of same-sex attracted representation, and in doing so dilute misinformation from groups who seek to capitalize on perpetuating stigma against same-sex attraction. This is also reflected in terms of US business leaders consistently reporting that they have difficulty with recruitment, retention and tourism in US states that debate or pass legislation that excludes LGBTQ+ people from full participation in daily life, and that includes the children of their valued employees and recruits (Human Rights Campaign 2022).

Consumer-focused brands and social narrative video

Negative reactions to co-option of social movements by consumer-focused brands, such as Gillette's 'The Best Men Can Be' campaign, show the continued intersectional significance of networked misogyny, stigma against same-sex attraction, and manosphere responses to challenges to conventional masculinity (Trott 2020).

Gillette's Best Men Can Be campaign speaks directly to the commodification of masculinity, gender politics, and the online networked partisanship indicative of the range of responses to the #MeToo movement. Responses to the The Best Men Can Be campaign are part of a broader public debate on the commodification of identity and the tribalism of digital protest, such as the divisive 2018 Nike campaign featuring US National Football League player Colin Kaepernick, and contention over representations and ownership of female body image in the 2019 Peloton advertisement 'The Gift That Gives Back'.

Gillette launched its 'We Believe' video, the first in its The Best Men Can Be campaign in January 2019. Negative responses claimed that the video was 'virtue signalling', 'political correctness', and 'wokeness' as a form of both. The 'boycott Gillette' hashtag reflects the segmented responses to representations of diverse sexualities and the conduct that might need to be addressed to ameliorate representational harms as a manifestation of ongoing bigotry. That video has been dissected by psychologists (Bogen et al 2021), marketing academics (Milfeld and Flint 2021) and masculinity scholars (Nebeling Petersen and Hvidtfeldt 2020).

Nebeling Petersen and Hvidfeldt (2020, p 13) argue that in the 'new' organization of masculinity represented in the 'We Believe' advertisement that 'men save women and fatherly figures teach boys how to behave in relation to other men and to the gendered other (the woman)'. They argue that this representation has recoded masculinity 'from toxicity to empathy without questioning the patriarchal organization in which women still are left outside the organization as mere objects for male-to-male action and intervention' (Nebeling Petersen and Hvidtfeldt 2020, p 13).

At the same time, they consider the notion that some of the negative reaction to the 'We Believe' video might be driven by the point that '[t]he recoding of masculinity from being characterized by inter-male violence, bullying and competition to one of inter-male care, support and empathy runs the risk of being framed as too homosocial, as gay, and this might explain why the ad neither mentions or represents male homosexuality nor challenges the boundaries of male-to-male desire' (Nebeling Petersen and Hvidtfeldt 2020, p 14).

Despite the criticism of Gillette's 'We Believe' video and the broader The Best Men Can Be campaign as sanctimonious and implausible from a global consumer goods brand, and an alleged hit to Procter and Gamble's bottom line, Gillette continued with the campaign into 2019 with social media and a narrative video launched on Facebook in May 2019 called 'First Shave'. In that video, transgender Toronto-based artist Samson Bonkeabantu Brown is shaving with some coaching from his father. The tagline for the video is 'Whenever, wherever, however it happens – your first shave is special' (Durkin 2019). The video of Bonkeabantu Brown's 'first shave' speaks to the ongoing commodification and segmentation of diverse masculinities. It also speaks to aspects of the human capabilities approach to agency that aims to secure freedoms from violence and discrimination for LGBT people and the reduced health and education outcomes associated with syndemic vulnerability, and which might be further achieved through positive media representation.

Conclusion

This chapter has contextualized the relationship between digital knowledge production processes, misrecognition of same-sex attraction and homophobia, and the broadening of LGBTQ+ cultural representation in popular culture and advertising as one strategy to minimize representational harms. In doing so, the chapter has aimed to develop thinking on the complex relationship between LGBTQ+ (mis)representation in popular culture and advertising and sexual citizenship research on LGBTQ+ recognition and redistribution to minimize representational harms. The chapter has also considered the reasoning behind continued stigma of same-sex attraction, and the relationship between misogyny and violence against gay men – a possible manifestation of masculine gender role discrepancy stress. The chapter has argued that increasing consideration of same-sex attraction as identity rather than sexual conduct has intersected with increased LGBTQ+ representation through streaming and social narrative videos by major corporations to increase positive representations of LGBTQ+ identification (Nielsen 2021). The next chapter analyses broader approaches to LGBTQ+ organizing.

FIVE

Digiqueer Activism, Advocacy and Allyship

Introduction

The hybrid media ecosystem has provided LGBTQ+ individuals and communities with new knowledge creation and networking opportunities for organizing (Corey 2019). This ongoing integration of the social and the digital allows citizens and consumers to quickly organize, assemble and vocalize support or express dissent through digital platforms (Armano 2017) to combat the stigmatic legacies and current realities of LGBTQ+ criminalization and pathologization.

That shift has generated new rituals of LGBTQ+ organizing through hashtag activism, crowdfunding advocacy through ecommerce, and philanthropy through non-fungible tokens (NFTs). Underscoring this digital connectivity are decades of LGBTQ+ organizing through protest and law reform, and in the US in particular, adversarial legalism, to secure relationship, conduct and expression rights. Central to those forms of organizing are protest-turned-pride events that drive economic enfranchisement of LGBTQ+ cultural representation through tourism within the growing annual public relations calendar of LGBTQ+ days and weeks of significance.

Amid the growth of online queer LGBTQ+ activism, advocacy and allyship, the gay bar as an organizing centre that enabled gay liberation movements and agendas (Lin 2021) – visibility, equal rights and protections under the law, equal access to healthcare, employment and consumer services – can now be found in Facebook threads, TikTok videos, WhatsApp groups, and to a lesser extent, awareness-raising campaigns and fundraising through dating apps.

Digital media platforms and their inadequate governance are a constant catalyst for LGBTQ+ organizing against representational harms, given the range of vulnerabilities LGBTQ+ communities face, calls for accountability, and an understanding of advocates' contributions to policy development (Gen and Wright 2013). Integral to those calls is identifying the extent to which effective advocacy is the result of a strong enough lobby with sufficient resources for campaigning (Solanke 2017).

This chapter synthesizes practitioner and academic literature on digital LGBTQ+ organizing. In doing so, the chapter analyses the ways that activists, advocates, and allies can 'queer it up' through policy and participatory advocacy against challenges to diverse LGBTQ+ expression through hybrid media. This is reflected in how sexual minorities have sought to define LGBTQ+ normative modes of embodiment, risk and disposability (Kafer and Grinberg 2019) on, and in, their own terms, through knowledge production processes from the late 1960s and subsequent decades to the present.

The chapter considers where LGBTQ+ networked identities sit within the digital organizing landscape. On one level, political insecurity through the 'hate feedback loop' (Bjork-James 2019) keeps LGBTQ+ organizers in the policy 'trenches' (Castells 2010) as they maintain the fight for basic relationship, expression and conduct rights that the general public might take for granted. On another level, increased recognition of LGBTQ+ expression through popular culture, relationship rights such as same-sex marriage (Hart-Brinson 2016), and social networks, sees a related expansion of the social imagination of homosexuality as identity rather than conduct across health and welfare, religion, immigration, securitization, markets, nationalism, a sense of belonging and other identifiers (Richardson 2018). As such, LGBTQ+ mobilization through campaigning continues to pursue broader recognition that can mitigate the stigma of criminalization and pathologization of same-sex attraction and related gender diversity. As shown throughout this book, the effects across and within jurisdictions and digital platforms are uneven.

This chapter firstly defines key terms before discussing legal, medical and economic approaches to LGBTQ+ advocacy and digital methods to achieve LGBTQ+ recognition. In doing so, the chapter synthesizes practitioner and academic literature in the pracademic tradition (Piza et al 2021) to provide a snapshot of LGBTQ+ organizing tactics, underscored by ongoing legal and medical reforms.

Digiqueering it up: defining the three As of digital LGBTQ+ organizing

Political opportunity structures and social and cultural events provide varied opportunities for political, economic and social organizing to realize LGBTQ+ relationship, conduct and expression rights (Richardson 2018). As such, the breadth of individual and group LGBTQ+ organizing in the context of Web 2.0 participation benefits from a broad definition – a process of coordinating task goals and activities to resources. To narrow this focus I have conceptualized digital LGBTQ+ organizing under the 'three As' of activism, advocacy, and allyship.

Activism can be defined as an action on behalf of a cause that goes beyond what is conventional or routine (Anderson and Herr 2007). This definition speaks to the 'vigorous' nature of campaigning to bring about political or social change in conventional definitions of activism. This 'vigour' can be used by proponents to argue that status quo approaches to injustice without vigour perpetuate status quo inequity, and by critics to imply that any vigorous challenge to the status quo involves some form of injury. The tension between these definitions speaks to the power of rhetoric in framing public debate through varied vocabulary to define aspects of organizing, such as protests, rallies, marches, civil disobedience and riot. However, it has often been direct action through protest in conjunction with legal claims of discrimination through the LGBTQ+ identity politics movement that has secured recognition for LGBTQ+ rights (Mason 2014).

A general definition of *advocacy* is 'public support for or recommendation of a particular cause or policy' (Oxford Dictionaries 2015, np). However, in practice this definition might be narrowed to intentional activities initiated by the public to affect policy and/or the policy-making process (Gen and Wright 2013). *Allyship* can be defined as 'active support for the rights of a minority or marginalized group without being a member of it' (New Oxford American Dictionary 2022, np). There is clearly possible overlap between aspects of these definitions, notable in what might constitute 'active' in the definition of ally, for example, and in the co-option of 'activism' as a pejorative by primary definers such as politicians. There can also be contradictions between corporate conduct in relation to lack of protection of LGBTQ+ expression from representational harms at the user level through inadequate moderation, and support for LGBTQ+ recognition and redistribution at the corporate level through philanthropy and organizational responses that visibly support LGBTQ+ representation.

LGBTQ+ policy and participatory advocacy

The modern gay and lesbian interest groups emerging in the early 1970s were representative of a larger turn in 'civic life away from federated mass membership organizations and toward the more donor-dependent professional advocacy firms and non-profits that characterize interest group politics today' (Wuest 2021, p 841). The spectrum of that organizing has included

programmatic (or issue) advocacy – when an organization takes a position on a public policy that affects their work;

legislative advocacy, or lobbying of legislators; political campaign activity to support or oppose political candidates; demonstrations [to] rally public support around an issue or policy; boycotts to encourage or discourage business with a targeted entity; and litigation, or using legal action to advance a cause. (Gen and Wright 2013, p 165)

In Australia, a snapshot by decade (see Willett 2000) suggests that political action was not seriously considered in the 1950s, however by the late 1960s decriminalization was on the minds of politicians, clergy, newspaper editors and liberal reformers (Willett 2000). In 1970 the first gay rights organizations were established, and since then political activism has been a permanent part of Australian homosexual life, putting and keeping gay issues firmly on the public agenda (Willett 2000). The 1980s saw a shift in gay politics around AIDS activism, and gays, lesbians and queers as knowledge producers through the emergence of gay and lesbian media, festivals and service organizations of its own (Willett 2000).

These developments owed much to both the business quest for the 'gay dollar', and to activists, 'who set out to make the emerging gay subculture into a community, with real political and social clout' (Willett 2000, p xi). Baird has noted the shift in focus to relationship rights in Australia since the late 1990s. Juxtaposing the campaigning for marriage equality in Australia with 'activism' for LGBTQI asylum seeker politics, she notes the signification of 'the systematic and increasingly institutionally engaged nature of marriage politics and the smaller, less systematic and less sustained political support for asylum seekers' (and of the limits of homonormativity in current contexts) (Baird 2018, p 476).

The tactical foundations of LGBTQ+ digital organizing to ward off representational harms such as 'algorithmic annihilation' (Karizat et al 2021) can range from policy to participatory advocacy, and might extend to activism and/or allyship. The primary aim of policy advocacy is a change in policy or the policy-making process. The primary aim of participatory advocacy is to make the policy process more accessible and transparent (Gen and Wright 2013). This distinction is pertinent when analysing representational harms against LGBTQ+ expression given that access to big-tech decision-making processes remains a constant source of criticism, despite greater oversight of ethics through measures such as Facebook's oversight board. The mix of top-down policy advocacy and bottom-up participatory advocacy is particularly well suited, and is mutually constituted, through the hybrid media ecosystem. As such, at the individual user level, much of the advocacy engaged in is participatory, such as hashtag activism, (covered in more detail below), and which reflects the capacity of Web 2.0 technologies for engagement.

The unpredictability of digital media can mobilize latent participatory advocacy, notable with the first use of the phrase 'MeToo' by Tarana Burke in 2006, and the global phenomenon that is now the MeToo movement through the viral #MeToo hashtag in 2017. As such, the role of the individual is very much central to hybrid media advocacy and clearly impactful through the rise of social media influencers. However, to go beyond 'slacktivism' within online interpretive communities – performative engagement such as liking, sharing or commenting – a digital presence needs to be connected to a broader cause that can harness the call to action. For example, by directing users to mutual aid funds and protest guides which can lead to real-time change, and which can include hashtag activism. An omission of a cause and a call to action is reflected in the lack of engagement with the #pridefall hashtag used by anti-LGBTQ+ manosphere proponents during Pride month.

As noted in the introduction, the diversification of digital media can expose 'flaktivism' in unidirectional traditional news media – the notion that politically insecure groups such as LGBTQ+ are granted visibility in news media to the extent that they can support the status quo through providing false balance, while those media companies profit from the structural disadvantage of the status quo and at the same time seem progressive (Corey 2019; see also Herman and Chomsky).

In empirical research on Black Lives Matter organizing, social media has been particularly useful for participatory activism through mobilizing new activists at scale, for meaning making though shaping public discourse and amplifying narratives, and for generating cross-movement coalitions within a wider movement network (Mundt et al 2018). This coalition building might also broaden the frame of digiqueer activism to draw on 'the creation and maintenance of intersectional social justice movements that seek to improve the lives of racial and sexual minorities' (Swank and Fahs 2022, p 1954).

In terms of systemizing LGBTQ+ digital organizing, this chapter collates advocacy organizing strategies and tactics into four main groupings: (1) reform efforts; (2) coalition building; (3) information campaigning; (4) and policy monitoring (Gen and Wright 2013). These components of the organizing toolkit reflect the complexity of the policy-making process itself, with interacting considerations such as a lengthy time span, difficulties of attributing success to a particular organizing effort, and the central role of values (Sabatier 1999). It is to a finer grained analysis of LGBTQ+ organizing that this chapter now turns, drawing on these groupings and the spectrum of participatory and policy advocacy noted earlier.

Reform efforts

Legal

LGBTQ+ individual and collective responses to representational harms continue to invoke identity politics as a basis for law reform to address discrimination from criminal justice institutions (Mason 2014). Decriminalization of same-sex conduct has been an ongoing law reform effort across decades and across jurisdictions (Mason and Tomsen 1997, Mouzos and Thompson 2000, Tomsen 2002, Robinson 2008, Ellis

2021). For example, in Australia it took 22 years – from 1975 to 1997 – to decriminalize consensual same-sex conduct across all Australian jurisdictions (*Toonen* v *Australia* [1994]).

Subsequently, the insertion of a clause in the marriage act in 2004 to define marriage as between a man and a woman (Marriage Amendment Act 2004 (Cth)) resulted in a 13-year advocacy campaign to secure same-sex marriage rights, which were finally enacted in Australia in 2017 (Robinson and Greenwich 2018, Betts and Bennett 2021).

Law reform efforts might also involve the repeal of 'homosexual advance defences', a legal strategy to defend or mitigate sentencing for criminal conduct in response to alleged unwanted same-sex sexual advances. In terms of removing the legal residues used to justify discrimination against consensual same-sex conduct, law reform also needs to include the expungement of decriminalized offences.

From a digiqueer perspective, the decriminalization of consensual same-sex conduct in Singapore in 2022, a jurisdiction with no sexual rights, means that LGBTQ+ young people will no longer have to evade state surveillance of homosexuality, while still drawing on social networks for allied friendships, romantic partners and safe communities (Yue and Lim 2022). However, same-sex marriage rights will continue to be denied.

Recent legal responses to algorithmic representational harms have included group, corporate and individual litigation. At the corporate level, Amazon-owned streaming platform Twitch filed suit against users who generate algorithmically driven racist, sexist, homophobic and transphobic 'hate raids' (*Twitch Interactive Inc* v *CruzzControl, CreatineOverdose* [2021]). As noted earlier, raids were intended as an engagement strategy in which Twitch streamers would point viewers toward another friendly account after their stream concluded to boost their audiences (Fabiani 2021); however, with 'hate' raids, trolls overwhelm streamers' chats with bot-powered fake accounts that spam hateful messages (Grayson 2021).

At the group level, in 2019 YouTube content creators filed a lawsuit against YouTube for engaging in discriminatory, anticompetitive and unlawful conduct that harms a protected class of persons under California law, claiming YouTube's recommendation algorithm demonetizes and hides content created by members of the LGBTQ+ community, among other claims (*LGBTQ+* v *Google Inc* [2020]). While not coordinated with LGBTQ+ advocacy groups, defamation cases might go some way to generating responses to inadequate moderation of online bias-motivated conduct against diverse LGBTQ+ individuals and communities, outside of US freedom of speech protections and within Australia's pro-complainant defamation context. See *Barilaro* v *Google LLC* [2022] FCA 650, which found YouTube liable as a publisher of user-generated content, once made aware of its defamatory nature.

The continuing exploitation of victims by Alex Jones, founder of conspiracy theory and far right fake news website Infowars, despite twice losing defamation suits in the US (Lewis 2022), one about baseless claims that the Sandy Hook shooting was a fiction, exemplifies the endemic nature of hate endorsed by digital platforms against vulnerable populations and the money to be made out of stigma-derived fictions. That case is indictive of a permissive political context in the US that has made denigrating victims part of political theatre. This example shows that while legal processes might effect justice in certain contexts, that hate will continue to thrive while online platforms facilitate misinformation, and allow people like Jones to still use their platforms for ecommerce to sustain their fictions (Lewis 2022).

In terms of holding traditional news media companies to account, Dominion Voting Systems defamation case against Fox News Network that alleges the cable TV network amplified false claims that Dominion voting machines were used to rig the 2020 US presidential election against Republican Donald Trump, and in favor of his Democratic rival Joe Biden, who won the election, is set to define newsworthiness and responsibility for misinformation within the broader instability of the hybrid media ecosystem (*US Dominion, Inc.* v *Fox News Network*, LLC 2021).

At the same time, Keck (2009) argues that despite the backlash to courtroom victories for LGBTQ+ rights provoking conservative counter-mobilization, that such victories through legal mobilization have sometimes been a promising avenue for pursuing policy changes whose prospects were otherwise quite limited. This argument can be seen in the consolidation of Drag Queen Storytime into a non-profit organization in the US in response to networked protest, and the clarification of aspects of public library governance. However, antagonistic legislative proposals that restrict resourcing of public libraries and threaten librarians with jail terms speak to the potential chilling effect on expression that might eventuate at the same time. The current legislative attack on LGBTQ+ people and communities in the US will test Keck's argument across US states at scale.

Conversely, Russell (2020, p 119) has argued that knowledgeable and mobilized queer movements 'that elicit formal apologies have been more successful than anti-hate crime activism in drawing attention to systemic harms perpetrated by powerful institutions of law, medicine and policing'. Russell notes the shortcomings, for example, of hate crime campaigns that 'may redirect public attention away from structural patterns of social marginalization that cannot be effectively framed in individual terms' (2020, p 113). These symbolic gestures speak to the power of non-punitive reparative approaches to LGBTQ+ cultural representation that might amplify positive framing of LGBTQ+ expression through popular culture, and that in turn might build allyship through 'dissonant identity priming' (Harrison and Michelson 2017), as will be further discussed.

Medical

In terms of harnessing allies from medicine to the LGBTQ+ depathologization cause, Wuest (2021) has shown how biomedical and mental health institutions and ideas have become foundational to the character of US LGBTQ+ advocacy and campaigns for equal rights, and arguably across many jurisdictions (ILGA World 2020a). Conflict 'over conversion therapy bans offer a view into how scientists, non-profit leaders, litigators and activists have worked together to construct and deploy increasingly biological conceptions of sexual and gender identities from the mid-20th century to the present' (Wuest 2021, p 838).

Wuest (2021) links recent legislative and litigation campaigns to ban conversion therapy for sexual orientation and gender identity and argues that '[i]n championing such bans, the American LGBTQ+ advocacy movement has incorporated its extensive network of scientific and medical allies into legal arguments, legislative testimonies, educational materials and political cultural discourse' (Wuest 2021, p 838). At the same time, Wuest notes that, despite the clear power and success of a medical and mental health focus, it has also led to overextensions of scientific authority and epistemology; overextensions 'that have consequences for gender and sexual autonomy, self-determination, and democratic governance that extend both from the principles and political commitments of liberal pluralists and adherents of more postmodern traditions like queer theory' (Wuest 2021, p 839).

Algorithms that drive same-sex attracted people to 'rabbit holes' of inaccurate online information about 'conversion therapy' speak to the invocation of 'science' as a justification for ongoing representational harms against same-sex attraction. This stigma can perpetuate homophobia that includes motivating individuals to transition, and detransition, when they cannot reconcile their same-sex attraction through that process (Littman 2021).

In research that speaks to the power of identity affiliation for LGBTQ+ young people through online participation, research into why youth of different sexual orientations look for sexual health information online found that 19 per cent of heterosexual youth and 78 per cent of gay/lesbian/queer youth looked for sexual health information online (Mitchell et al 2014). The most common reasons that youth look for sexual health information online is for privacy and curiosity. Youth from sexual minorities are more likely than heterosexual youth to report that they looked for information online because they did not have anyone to ask (Mitchell et al 2014). It is notable, that '[o]nce youth have the information, no differences by sexual orientation were noted as to what they did with it. Instead, seeking out the information for privacy-related reasons and having no one to ask were related to taking some action on the information received' (Mitchell et al 2014, p 147). Findings from that research 'indicate that online information is most valuable to those youth who lack alternatives, and which may include rural and regional LGBTQ+ populations' (Mitchell et al 2014, p 147). As such, care needs to be taken to ensure that sexual health information online is accurate and includes topics specific to sexual minorities (Mitchell et al 2014).

Economic coalition building

As noted earlier, the transformation of cultural production through digital media platforms has restructured the terms by which culture is distributed and paid for (Caplan and Gillespie 2020). In research documenting consumer initiatives to support victims and victims' families after the Pulse nightclub shooting in Orlando in 2016, Corey has considered 'the cultural problematics and political limitations present in the joining of socio-political critique with commodity activism and the investments and consequences for LGBTQ+ communities' (Corey 2019, p 119).

Within relatively well-organized LGBTQ+ communities with a capacity to effectively mobilize quickly, ethical purchasing and hiring decisions can be harnessed to challenge prejudice through consumer activism and advocacy, using and/or withholding purchasing power to exert influence in ways that work for social change (Corey 2019). Ethical consumers use purchasing power to make social and political statements.

Citizen–consumers vote in product (not just civic) campaigns. These categories may be mutually constitutive, and as such the ethical/citizen consumer should be a both/and consideration to reflect the complex choices that consumers and allies make about their identity (Corey 2019). This complexity is also reflected in the composition of pride parades that include major corporations, and policing organizations that have discriminated, and in cases still do, against LGBTQ+ people and communities, and corporations that publicly advocate for LGBTQ+ communities but that donate funds to political campaigns by anti-LGBTQ+ lawmakers.

Consumer boycotts serve as models of protest in advocacy for LGBTQ+ rights, among other vulnerable groups. The power of the 'gaycott' is possibly most notable in the recognition by major corporations that they have difficulty with recruitment, retention and tourism in US states that debate or pass legislation that excludes LGBTQ+ people from full participation in daily life (Human Rights Campaign 2022). This is in addition to a range of crowdfunding initiatives that have been shut down on the basis of discrimination against LGBTQ+ peoples.

In addition to boycott strategies, LGBTQ+ organizations such as the Human Rights Campaign and the Australian Workplace Equality Index produce annual ratings of corporate treatment of LGBTQ+ employees. The scores from such indexes 'help consumers make informed decisions on where and how to exercise their purchasing power in support of LGBTQ+ rights' (Corey, p 122). At the same time, 'consumers can purchase a variety of commodities from some of these organizations, such as tote bags, cup holders, hats, t-shirts and other goods, with proceeds from these sales funding 'a variety of programmes and advocacy campaigns for LGBTQ+ rights' (Corey, p 122). As such, 'political aspirations are projected onto commodities and, simultaneously, citizenship activities are commodified' (Corey 2019, p 124).

The recognition of same-sex marriage in the US and the recognition of the value of the 'rainbow family' as a market segment might generate further recognition through greater screen presence and the quality of that screen presence (Nielsen 2021), and to distributive effects through tolerance and acceptance. As such, the notion of LGBTQ+ individuals and communities as early adopters and more frequent users of technology continues, and has some salience. For example, while streaming is part of everyday life for all Americans, 85 per cent of LGBTQ+ people reported that they had used a video streaming service in the last 30 days, compared with 74 per cent for the general population (Nielsen 2021).

In terms of amplifying positive representation through campaigning that might harness allies to broaden LGBTQ+ institutional legitimacy through relationship rights such as same-sex marriage, and 'rainbow families', Harrison and Michelson (2017) argue that 'dissonant identity priming' can result in allyship, where seemingly unrelated in-group identities effectively develop feelings of interpersonal closeness and open minds to attitudinal change. The argument goes that they can do this 'by leveraging the power of group membership and by generating cognitive "speed bumps" that motivate recipients to be attentive to delivered messages' (Harrison and Michelson 2017, p 6):

> In other words, if you can induce a person to believe they are speaking with or hearing from a member of a mutually identifying group (e.g., someone from their shared ethno-racial group or political party), they should be more likely to engage in a conversation and to be more open to attitude change, even on contentious political and social issues. Counter-stereotypical or dissonant messages, because they are unexpected, should garner more attention and thus be more effective. (Harrison and Michelson 2017, p 18)

This notion is reflected in advertising research in 'modern societies' with high levels of wealth and education that develop a higher level of social trust. This can in turn reduce 'minority stereotypes and offsets the negative impact of any perceived threats through high diversity in society' (Eisend and Hermann 2019, p 382). At the same time, '[i]ncreasing positive reactions of majority consumers toward minority portrayals in advertising correlate with increasing acceptance, visibility, and support for minority groups in society' (Eisend and Hermann 2019, p 382).

At the intersection of employment market forces and alternatives to legal advocacy to combat criminal conduct against LGBTQ+ peoples is the Global Index on Legal Recognition of Homosexual Orientation (GILRHO) (Badgett et al 2019). This data set enumerates the costs of violence against same-sex attraction through economic harms such as 'lost labour time, lost productivity, underinvestment in human capital, and the inefficient allocation of human resources through discrimination in education and hiring practices', and which makes the case for the mutual reinforcement of LGBT inclusion and economic development (Badgett et al 2019, p 12).

Pride as economic and social capital

Pride-turned-protest movements have invoked economic arguments, about tourism revenue in particular, as a lever for greater police accountability and integration of LGBTQ+-friendly policies (Ellis 2021). It is in this way that the intermittent nature of coalition building sustains the visibility of the LGBTQ+ initialism throughout the annual rainbow events calendar (such as World AIDS Day, Wear It Purple etc).

Annual demonstrations-turned-pride events show the return on investment of decades of LGBTQ+ advocacy in political and economic terms, and as a forum through which to challenge episodic representational harms against LGBTQ+ agency (Marsh and Galbraith 1995). In doing so, the ongoing commodification of LGBTQ+ public protests into celebrations of diversity (Marsh and Galbraith 1995) reflects the economic imperatives that might broaden interest in LGBTQ+ recognition and redistribution beyond those communities as their sexual citizenship gains greater mainstream legitimacy (Richardson 2017).

For example, the origins of the Sydney Gay and Lesbian Mardi Gras Parade as a public protest against discrimination against gay men and lesbians in the 1970s, and in solidarity with other gay and lesbian communities around the world, is central to its symbolic significance (Marsh and Galbraith 1995). It is within this context that, for example, the Sydney Gay and Lesbian Mardi Gras as a social movement contributed to the differentiation of 'citizen political identities' of the gay and lesbian community, and the normalization of these identities through political mobilization (Marsh and Galbraith 1995, p 300).

The popularity, visibility and scale of the Sydney Gay and Lesbian Mardi Gras 'has given it a vanguard role both in the development of a gay and lesbian community and in relations between this community and the wider society' (Marsh and Galbraith 1995, p 301). This status highlights the significance of the Sydney Gay and Lesbian Mardi Gras Parade as a reflection of the moral and social issues of the day. The Sydney Gay and Lesbian Mardi Gras also reflects the Sydney gay and lesbian community's ability to mobilize 'reasonable' numbers for particular events and demonstrations. Marsh and Galbraith (1995, p 310) suggest that the Mardi Gras' 'impact on public, media and political opinion' is arguably its most important and strategic extra-community influence. At the same time, the parade and related LGBTQ+ events throughout the annual Sydney Mardi Gras Festival provide significant economic and social benefits to the local and national economy (Wotherspoon 2016).

The continued presence of major corporations at pride parades reflects the continued mainstreaming of diverse LGBTQ+ expression, the role of some of those corporations in addressing economic discrimination against diverse communities and people, and the alignment of brands to social issues noted in Chapter 4. From the annual June Pride festival celebrated in many countries (February/March for the Sydney Gay and Lesbian Mardi Gras), LGBTQ+ 'days of significance' have burgeoned, and reflect the growing recognition of diverse LGBTQ+ sexualities and the spread of events throughout the year: 1988 World AIDS Day (December); 1990 IDAHOBIT (May); 1999 Celebrate Bisexuality Day (September); 1999 Transgender Day of Remembrance (November); 2008 Lesbian Visibility Day (May); and 2010 Wear it Purple (August). At the same time, the tension over representation in pride parades, particularly of uniformed police (Cockburn 2020), and major corporations, amid claims of 'rainbow washing' – using or adding rainbow colours and/or imagery to advertising, apparel, landmarks etc, to indicate progressive support for LGBTQ+ equality with minimum effort or outcome (Urban Dictionary 2023, np) – reflect the political purchase of inclusion in parades and marches that are increasingly made for streaming audiences.

As noted in Chapter 2, in terms of 21st century neoliberal capitalists working within the technocracy, Valocchi (2017, p 316) argues that they have 'generated a class fraction of finance and digital capitalists' that has given dominant social movement organizations tremendous economic resources to build national professional organizations, in the US at least.

Information campaigning

Information campaigning is a major component of the LGBTQ+ organizing strategies noted throughout this book. Organizations such as LGBT Tech encourage the continued early adoption and use of cutting-edge, new and emerging technologies by providing information, education and strategic outreach for LGBT communities (LGBT Tech 2021). But there are few of these dedicated LGBTQ+ organizations.

The Electronic Frontier Foundation is the leading nonprofit organization defending civil liberties in the digital world, including the rights of LGBTQ+ (Electronic Frontier Foundation 2023).

Access Now defends and extends the digital rights of users at risk around the world through advocacy, grants for grassroots organizations and activist groups that are working with users and communities most at risk of digital rights violations, policy and in general awareness raising with a particular focus on privacy, freedom of expression, digital security, business and human rights and internet discrimination (Access Now 2021). The Australian Hate Crime Network provides resources for LGBTQ+ individuals and communities seeking to develop their awareness of these issues.

In terms of periodic and episodic data on the surveillance of LGBTQ+ peoples, the UN Independent expert on sexual orientation and gender identity has reported on data collection and management as a means to create heightened awareness of violence and discrimination based on sexual orientation and gender identity (Madrigal-Borloz 2019). The issues facing LGBTQ+ organizers across a range of jurisdictions, including laws and regulations that prohibit media or web content as well as propaganda laws that prohibit the promotion of 'homosexuality' or 'non-traditional' sexual relations are regularly researched by ILGA and OutRight International (OutRight Action International 2018, ILGA World 2020b, Madrigal-Borloz 2021, OutRight Action International 2021).

The Insikt Group frames its research into censorship and discrimination against LGBTQIA+ individuals and groups through 'cyber threat analysis' (Insikt Group 2021, Insikt Group 2022). The digital particulars of so-called 'conversion therapies' are documented in detail by the Global Project Against Hate and Extremism (ILGA World 2020a, Global Project Against Hate and Extremism 2022a, 2022b). Parliamentary debates remain a source of topical issues (House of Lords and House of Commons 2021), as do reports by eSafety commissioners (eSafety Commissioner 2021).

The breadth of ways to display representational harms include an interactive Atlas of Hate Map from Poland, which currently ranks among the lowest of all nations in Europe regarding LGBTQIA+ rights. At least a third of the country has been declared an 'LGBT Free Zone' on the Atlas of Hate Map (https://atlasnienawisci.pl/), which effectively visualizes the stigmatization. The maps creators were nominated for the Sakharov Prize for Freedom of Thought granted by the European Parliament. This is the second ever case of an organization being nominated for opposing the authorities in a member state of the EU.

The Equaversity Foundation was established in Poland in 2021 to organize a worldwide fundraising effort to benefit the LGBT+ community in Poland and neighbouring countries. Its goal is to provide financial support to local groups on the ground that serve as front-line defenders in various sections of the country, often in small, local communities. A number of Polish organizations have been formed and are ready to help in this regard. However, in 2020, the activists were also sued by several local governments supported by Ordo Iuris, ultra-conservative Polish Catholic legal organization and think tank, for infringement of personal rights.

Monitoring

Fact checking remains vital to countering attacks from anti-LGBTQ+ groups, as seen earlier in cases relating to false information about Drag Queen Storytime personnel and a presenter (Funke 2022, Swenson 2022) or in the situations that follow. Public shaming exercises such as Sleeping Giants, a social media activism organization that aims to pressure companies into removing advertisements from controversial conservative news outlets, has become routine, and as such might straddle the activist and advocacy divide.

Media Matters in the US works daily to notify activists, journalists, pundits, and the general public about instances of misinformation, providing them with the resources to rebut false claims, and to take direct action against offending media institutions. In an LGBTQ+ keyword search of Media Matters, and in line with the recent renewed conflation of male same-sex attraction with 'grooming' of children, the first four mentions from August 2022 feature grooming in relation to same-sex attraction.

In response to the malicious use of the term 'groomer' to spread unfounded accusations of child abuse against LGBTQ+ people, Twitter banned the targeted use of the term (Gingerich 2022). It was in response to the Twitter ban that Tim Pool took to his YouTube channel with over 1 million subscribers to make his claim that the LGBTQ+ community had been 'taken over' by paedophiles (Gingerich 2022) and which was still online nearly a week after Media Matters reported it, having accumulated more than a quarter of a million views (Gingerich 2022).

Collaborative journalists and 'solutions journalism' organizations of that name have a role to play in constructive reporting, for example, featuring positive stories about LGBTQ+ experience such as support for LGBTQ+ refugees in Denmark, and calls from medical students for more LGBT health training to address disparities. This author has relied on a freedom of information (FOI) request to determine the legal costs of unlawful police conduct at the 2013 Sydney Gay and Lesbian Mardi Gras (Ellis 2021), and media outlets pursue FOI requests regularly to expose structural harms (Taylor 2020).

Counterpublic digital activism

Online communities play a major role in monitoring and direct action to address algorithmic and content-based representational harms through 'counterpublic digital activism': activism enacted by 'counterpublic-subordinated' social groups that are in contrast with the 'public', the dominant cultural form. However, the 'value of counterpublic communication is rarely recognized, except by those seeking to change the status quo' (Renninger 2015, p 1514). This is because counterpublic communication engages in the 'non-compliant practices of intervening, and the formation of new social and cultural structures, both in support of and resistance to changing social norms and values' (Lindtner et al 2011, pp 5–6). Yet, this activism can generate longer-term outcomes, as noted above, if for example, it directs users to mutual aid funds and protest guides which can lead to real-time change, and which can include hashtag activism.

Schudson and van Anders (2019) have researched Tumblr's unique capacity to formulate networked counterpublics due to 'features such as accessible private and anonymous interactions, relative equivalence of content generated by new and experienced users, and the use of hashtags to consolidate content and make it easily searchable' (Schudson and van Anders 2019, p 355). They find that asexual, queer and trans young people (AQTYP) 'engage with gender and sexual identity discourses in online counterpublics in ways that challenge many, but not all, parameters of hegemonic identity discourses' (Schudson and van Anders 2019, p 354). They argue that 'new understandings of sexuality and gender in AQTYP's networked counterpublics are a form of queer world-making in which the feelings and relationalities that constitute sexual and gendered subjectivities cannot be considered self-evident, stable, or universal' (Schudson and van Anders 2019, p 354).

An example of how the instability of digital platforms intersects with the mediated negotiation of identity online is transgender interaction with hashtags on Twitch, and the unanticipated conversion of raids into a tactic of hate. Raids were set up by Twitch as an engagement strategy where Twitch streamers would point viewers toward another friendly account after their stream concluded to boost their audiences (Fabiani 2021) at the behest of transgender streamers. This made it easier for transgender streamers to build their communities, and to discover content that resonates with them on the platform (Fabiani 2021). However, as previously discussed, with 'hate' raids, trolls overwhelm streamers' chats with bot-powered fake accounts that spam hateful messages (Grayson 2021).

Three primary themes emerged from McInroy et al's research into online fandom communities (OFC) as networked counterpublics: '(1) that LGBTQ+ mass media narratives remained insufficient but were improving; (2) counternarratives produced within OFCs were even better; however, (3) the climate of OFCs created challenges and limitations, including to the quantity and quality of depictions of diverse LGBTQ+ identities' (McInroy et al 2022, p 629). It is to a deeper discussion of online queer fandom hashtag activism, and algorithmic resistance, that the chapter now turns.

Hashtag activism and algorithmic resistance

In contrast to the mass media's continued deficiencies in the depiction of LGBTQ+ people and communities, '[o]nline fandom communities (OFCs) provide lesbian, gay, bisexual, transgender, queer, and other sexual and/or gender minority (LGBTQ+) youth opportunities to access community-generated LGBTQ+ representations' (McInroy et al 2022, p 629). As such, digital 'queer fan hashtag campaigns respond to shifts in industrial practice that have increased the value of fans, social media, and fans on social media' (Navar-Gill and Stanfill 2018, p 85).

In terms of the mutual constitution of strategic online engagement that seeks to address representational inequity through hashtag activism, queer fan hashtag campaigns can harness affordances and industrial values through stating what is wrong in industrial practice and what they articulate as a better way (Navar-Gill and Stanfill 2018). Such campaigns 'are strategic interventions meant to alter both representational and structural television production processes by leveraging the importance of audience feedback in a connected viewing environment' (Navar-Gill and Stanfill 2018, p 85).

In research on identity negotiation, Karizat and others (2021) have analysed qualitative in-depth interviews with a small sample of TikTok users (n=15) to evaluate the workings of 'algorithmic resistance': intentional behaviours to produce algorithmic outcomes different from what would otherwise be produced, to combat what they call 'algorithmic symbolic annihilation' – algorithms that further 'normative and reductive understandings of phenomena and identities, rendering some invisible and marginalized' including LGBTQ identity, to counter algorithmic representational harm (Karizat et al 2021, p 3). The point of the resistance is to achieve representational belonging – 'the positive emotional response to seeing members of one's community and its intricacies represented' (Karizat et al 2021, p 3).

Doxing

In terms of the broader application of digital terms and their contestation, Anderson and Wood have noted that doxing – 'the practice of publishing private, proprietary, or personally identifying information on the internet, usually with malicious intent' (Anderson and Wood 2021, p 205) – has become a testing ground for free speech, a battleground between right and left ideology, an affirmation of credibility in non-fungible tokens (NFT) and crypto communities, and a conceptualization of harm and harassment. As such, aspects of the tension between competing interests over privacy, anonymity and trust transcend the predigital and digital divide.

For example, typologies of doxing beyond intentional technology-facilitated violence can involve reputation-building and doxing in the public interest (Anderson and Wood 2021). These broader applications of doxing might benefit politically vulnerable communities through increasing scrutiny and accountability of disseminators of representational harms (Tiffany 2022). At the same time, media outlets and journalists who do this are not above reproach. However, the Facebook oversight board's recommendations, and Meta's adoption of most of those recommendations to limit recourse for Facebook users that dox other users, and to punish the doxers, is a recognition of the increased risk that vulnerable digital media users, such as women, children, the LGBTQ community and religious minorities, can face and 'which can cause a lot of emotional and physical distress, loss of employment, and in some extreme cases, termination of employment' (The Social Talks 2022, np).

Meta has said 'it won't take any actions against posts containing photos of the exterior of private residences except when they are posted with a malafide intent against the resident' (The Social Talks 2022, np). However, 'it will allow sharing the pictures of the exteriors of public offices of high-ranking officials, and will allow people to hold protests at those locations' (The Social Talks 2022, np). At the same time, the company did 'go against one of the board's recommendations and won't allow users to re-share the addresses of others who posted it on their will since it's impossible to know the intention of users who do so and it violates the consent of the ones who posted their address' (The Social Talks 2022, np).

Blockchain, cryptocurrencies and non-fungible tokens

The use of blockchain and related assets, such as NFTs and cryptocurrencies, have other purposes useful for LGBTQ+ recognition and redistribution, including philanthropy. In a furthering of commodification of diverse LGBTQ+ expression, organizations and individuals are engaging with NFTs to raise LGBTQ+ visibility, as a form of personalized self-expression, and as a digital asset. The main use of NFTs currently, however, is to support LGBTQ+ philanthropy through art auction fundraising (Simms 2022). For example, the Queenly NFT cryptogallery advances the work of queer creators, allowing patrons to invest by owning unique, digital collectibles such as NFTs (The Queenly NFT 2021). In June 2022, a Christie's auction of NFTs and physical artwork by 18-year-old transgender artist FEWOCiOUS (Victor Langlois) fetched US$2.16 million, the latest sign of appetite among art collectors for blockchain-based assets (Howcroft and Chavez-Dreyfuss 2021).

The Qtopia metaverse aims to provide an inclusive virtual space for the LGBTQ+ community, friends and allies to connect, while giving back to LGBTQ+ causes. Qtopia is being created with an emphasis on equality, diversity and sustainability.

While it is early days for cryptocurrencies, with the financial risks emphasized with the crash of FXT cryptocurrency exchange in 2022, they might offer increased financial accessibility given that almost anyone can own cryptocurrency without a credit score and in many cases without a photo ID (Newbery 2021), with fraud among other possible outcomes. At the same time, they might protect LGBTQ+ expression in jurisdictions where LGBTQ+ relationship, conduct and expression rights are restricted through criminal law, pathologization and stigmatization. The first LGBTQ+ cryptocurrency was launched in 2022, albeit with questions about its name – 'Maricoin', a wordplay on the Spanish word for 'faggot' (Street 2022).

In countries where same-sex marriage is not legal, it is extremely difficult for same-sex couples to access the same protections available to opposite-sex ones. The Famiee Project in Japan provides marriage certificates for same-sex couples in countries that have not legalized same-sex marriage (Lih Yi 2020). Famiee uses the blockchain to store these digital marriage certificates. Each entry on a blockchain ledger is anonymous and tamper-proof but can be accessed by those with the right permission. This means that couples can control who (if anyone) can view their information (Newbery 2021). The team has partnerships with insurance companies, banks and hospitals in Japan, where the project began. This way, same-sex couples can access some of the benefits – such as health insurance – that are open to opposite-sex couples.

Archival research

In terms of queering it up through LGBTQ+ cultural representation to accurately reflect the lived experience of queer identity, archival research is a possible site 'of recovery, a recuperative project of moving from silence to productive, transformative discourse' on LGBT sexual histories (Stone and Cantrell 2015, p 3). Stone and Cantrell apply the closet analogy to LGBT archival research in that the '[t]he archive, much like the closet, exposes various levels of publicness and privateness – recognition, awareness, refusal, impulse, disclosure, framing, silence, cultural intelligibility – each mediated and determined through subjective insider/outsider ways of knowing' (2015, p 3). At the same time, Ross (2017, p 269) has cautioned that '[t]he proper response to the indeterminacy of the sexual past is not to impose our own identities on it but to make new meanings out of it'. In terms of archival silences, Ross notes that

> To engage with the silences as they appear is not to be innocent of the present, either, but it is oriented toward contextualizing those silences themselves as revelatory of archival power. Recognizing the exclusions of the archives, then, does not necessarily require 'rescuing' individual histories from them, nor does it demand that we rework the archives to serve the needs of present-day communities. (2017, pp 273–4)

As noted earlier, Mary L. Gray has suggested qualitative research as a strategy to combat algorithmic bias against queer identities, and to qualify metrics; that ethnography is critical to understanding the contexts that shape aggregated data (Weber, 2020). Archival research presents a further opportunity to do this.

Conclusion

This chapter has provided a snapshot of the ways that activists, advocates and allies 'queer it up' through participatory and policy advocacy against challenges to diverse LGBTQ+ expression through hybrid media. This includes new rituals of

LGBTQ+ organizing through hashtag activism, crowdfunding advocacy, philanthropy through NFT, and the continued commodification of LGBTQ+ expression through ecommerce for advocacy and allyship. Emphasizing the importance of queer knowledge production in the fight for recognition, the chapter has connected the gay and lesbian political organizing from the late 1960s and subsequent decades to the marketization, professionalization, and individualization of political problems and solutions in late capitalism. The chapter has considered where LGBTQ+ networked expression sits within the digital organizing landscape. On the one hand, some LGBTQ+ organizers do remain in the policy trenches as mobilized recursive hate amplifies though social networks, and in response to the sheer scale of anti-LGBTQ+ adversarial litigation and legislation in the US at the moment. This is within the broader context of increased recognition of LGBTQ+ expression through popular culture, relationship rights such as same-sex marriage, and personal networks that see a related shift to recognition of homosexuality as identity rather than conduct. This shift has widened the window of representation for LGBTQ+ expression, and in doing so, has strengthened allyship that provides greater access to institutional legitimacy.

SIX

Data Driven Times?

Introduction

This book has identified a range of representational harms facing LGBTQ+ peoples within the hybrid media ecosystem of older and newer digital media logics – harms that denigrate, misrecognize, erase, or omit minority communities. I have conceptualized these harms as a form of information warfare that can perpetuate bias-motivated conduct across and through digital media platforms, and which can include algorithmic censorship, online vilification, such as slurs that minimize or conceal hate, and assault. This warfare is based on the manufacture of an imagined LGBTQ+ enemy, and the rationalization, normalization and monetization of stigma-driven marginaliziation based on that fiction. Through a range of case studies, the book has emphasized the atomistic nature of algorithmic intervention across jurisdictions, within a broader rise of violent domestic extremism that weaponizes diverse sexual and gender identity. Stigma against same-sex attraction, and its conflation with gender non-conformity, is often the basis for that weaponization. In doing so, the book has considered the consequences of representational harms on LGBTQ+ sites of legal, political and economic agency. The purpose of this chapter is to use the arguments laid out in the book as the jumping off point for consideration of current and future issues confronting the digiqueer in technocratic times.

The chapter considers the following four questions: (1) How will LGBTQ+ communities document, evaluate and disseminate their legal, political, and economic capital in response to representational harms? (2) How will big-tech companies respond to the 'techlash', which includes growing calls for regulation of digital platforms, and litigation that has found digital platforms responsible for representational harms such as defamatory content once made aware of it? (3) How will artificial intelligence such as ChatGPT perpetuate and ameliorate the structural biases against pre-digital LGBTQ+ expression through algorithmic discrimination, and responses to that discrimination noted throughout this book? (4) How will LGBTQ+ expression be impacted by information warfare in the grey zone – the space in between peace and war in which state and non-state actors engage in competition – as threats from digital technologies outside of physical war zones increase (Hayward 2020)? Before those questions are considered, the chapter summarizes the arguments and case studies drawn upon throughout.

Information warfare in technocratic times

Outlined in Chapter 1, this book has argued that lack of transparency over big tech and government decision-making, and blurred lines of privacy, consent and liability, have amplified hate against minority groups and individuals, including LGBTQ+. This ambiguity in turn amplifies representational harms against politically vulnerable communities through speculation that drives predation, such as vilification and assault, and the marginalization of LGBTQ+ expression through misrepresentation, censorship and omission – forms of structural violence present when somatic and mental realizations are below their potential (Galtung 1969, p 167).

Concurrently, adversarial news media framing of identity-based rights claims can pitch stakeholder groups against each other for perceived scarce resources – that one group's enfranchisement is another group's loss – and through slippery slope arguments based on sexual emergency rhetoric. This invocation has been seen in debates over same-sex marriage that involve a perceived loss of symbolic capital and moral authority for conservative and extremist ideologues. This framing does not recognize that enfranchisement of minority positions through broadening inclusion can minimize othering, and in doing so minimize the coercion that vulnerable populations can face through processes of stigmatization, which in turn can be used to justify decriminalization. Chapter 2 focused on the algorithmic representational harms that have inequitably sorted populations into measurable types for security and profit through surveillance technologies – a form of 'algorithmic governance' (Kafer and Grinberg 2019, p 596), perpetuating some of the structural biases against LGBTQ+ from pre-digital times. Algorithmically filtered, discriminatory depictions have reinforced the subordination of LGBTQ+ expression through stereotyping, recognition, denigration and underrepresentation (Mehrabi et al 2021). The monetization of bias through YouTube sites has included the sale of mundane items such as sweatshirts and mugs adorned with bias-driven homophobic slurs (Nett 2019).

Chapter 3 provided new insights into the mutual constitution of sexuality, gender, procreation, religion, and violent domestic extremism through the hybrid media ecosystem that amplifies hate against childhood literacy program Drag Queen Storytime (DQS). Protests against DQS have perpetuated bias-motivated conduct against LGBTQ+ expression through vilification, threats at protests, litigation, and the legislative process (Verrelli et al 2019, Donnelly-Drummond 2021).

As noted in Chapter 4, enumerating representational harms against same-sex attraction is significant given that '[d]epicting gay men as a threat to children may be the single most potent weapon for stoking public fears about homosexuality – and for winning elections and referenda in the US (The Southern Poverty Law Center 2011, np), and for related marginalization of LGBTQ+ in other jurisdictions.

This misrecognition is possible through the perpetuation of stigma against same-sex attraction through knowledge production processes that condone homophobia, and which at the same time have allowed for the broadening of LGBTQ+ cultural representation through popular culture as a strategy to minimize representational harms.

Chapter 5 synthesized practitioner and academic literature on LGBTQ+ organizing. In doing so, that chapter considered the ways that activists, advocates and allies 'queer it up' through participatory and policy advocacy against challenges to diverse LGBTQ+ expression. Political insecurity through the 'hate feedback loop' (Bjork-James 2019) keeps LGBTQ+ organizers in the policy 'trenches' (Castells 2010). At the same time, increased recognition of LGBTQ+ expression through popular culture, relationship rights such as same-sex marriage, and personal networks, see a related shift to recognition of homosexuality as identity rather than conduct. This shift widens the window of representation for LGBTQ+ expression, and in doing so strengthens allyship. As such, the book has provided new insight into the role of hybrid media knowledge production processes in developing LGBTQ+ cultural representation, the attribution of value to identity, and its purchase in securing LGBTQ+ relationship, conduct and expression rights.

The case studies throughout the book have spoken to the varied cultural contexts, formats and issues of digital media platforms and their governance, and LGBTQ+ experiences across those platforms. At the same time, co-option of the US civil rights notion of 'blindness' as a rhetorical device by conservative, premarket forces, has been mobilized to evade collective responsibility for the persistence of inequality (Solanke 2017). This has arguably resulted in the paradoxical sociological phenomenon of 'bigotry without bigots' that has flourished within unqualified protections of free speech in the US, and which the uncritical decontextualization of traditional news media framing can embolden.

Fighting in and beyond the trenches

The 'three As' of queer organizing noted in Chapter 5 – activism, advocacy and allyship – need to draw on a broad spectrum of support to maintain and secure LGBTQ+ relationship, conduct and expression rights into the hybrid future, and across jurisdictions. The digiqueer fight continues through law reform efforts to decriminalize same-sex relations, the pursuit of marriage equality (Ball et al 2019), advocacy to end 'conversion therapy' (ILGA World 2020a), and the unsettled nature of exemptions from anti-discrimination laws that protect LGBT people from service and employment discrimination on religious grounds (Richardson 2018; see also Elphick 2017, *Lee* v *Ashers Baking Company Ltd and others* [2018] UKSC 49, *Masterpiece Cakeshop, Ltd* v *Colorado Civil Rights Commission* [2018]).

Central to achieving these aims is the ongoing pursuit of comprehensive data on the world population affected by discrimination against diverse sexual orientation and gender identity. Such comprehensive data can be used to further justify allocation of resources to mitigate anti-LGBTQ+ stigmatic legacies through representational harms (Hudson-Sharp and Metcalf 2016, Park 2016, Madrigal-Borloz 2021), and which at the moment is fragmented and patchy at best.

Approximately sixty-seven United Nations (UN) member states still criminalize consensual same-sex conduct (ILGA World 2020a), with ongoing stigma concealing accurate numbers. In terms of the knowledge production processes that might generate and perpetuate representational harms, approximately forty-two UN member states have legal barriers for freedom of expression on issues related to sexual and gender diversity (ILGA World 2020b). Moreover, at least 51 UN member states have known legal barriers to the registration or operation of civil society organizations working on sexual and gender diversity issues (ILGA World 2020b). These provisions can include laws and regulations that prohibit media or web content, as well as propaganda laws that prohibit the promotion of 'homosexuality' or 'non-traditional' sexual relations. In many countries, governments have used domestic telecommunications companies to block pro-LGBTQ+ apps and websites (Insikt Group 2020). Further, law enforcement agencies have deployed the use of entrapment to expose members of the LGBTQ+ community for imprisonment and torture (Insikt Group 2020).

This intersection of tradition and the structural biases that have supported it are in stark contrast with the growing representation of, and identification with, LGBTQ+ identity that go beyond sexual conduct, amid a growing number of people who self-identify as LGBT or something other than heterosexual (Aurora and GiveOut 2022, Jones 2022). This growth of identification within growing decriminalization of same-sex conduct, expansion of marriage equality, and anti-discrimination law, may see further representational harms against these identifications as their visibility increases, and as violent reactions to the gender fluidity of Drag Queen Storytime childhood literacy events show.

In terms of methods, there is clearly value in triangulation of longitudinal macroeconomic data with health data to enumerate the syndemic vulnerabilities that LGBTQ+ individuals and groups face (Badgett et al 2019) through the legacies of criminalization and pathologization of same-sex conduct and related gender identities.

Media consumption data that enumerates LGBTQ+ screen presence and the quality of that presence speaks to the power of positive recognition and the potential to amplify the impact of 'dissonant identity priming' that can bring seemingly unrelated in-group identities together to effectively develop feelings of interpersonal closeness and open minds to attitudinal change (Harrison and Michelson 2017).

Combatting misinformation is central to combatting stigma as LGBTQ+ expression is caught up in the broader information war on truth. This is because two of the biggest challenges facing LGBTQ+ expression and ongoing harms of misrepresentation of same-sex attraction and related gender identity are the porosity of digital platforms, and their hosting of anti-LGBTQ+ hate and extremism.

The growth of groups that engage in anti-LGBTQ+ hate, their intersection with violent domestic extremists, and the relationship to misogyny requires further interrogation given the ongoing invocation of slurs that conflate same-sex male attraction with notions of femininity as a tactic of denigration. This is particularly the case given that many right-wing extremists today 'no longer subscribe to the narrow concept of nationalism but instead imagine themselves as participants in a global struggle against a global enemy', broadening the reach of nationalistic rhetoric beyond geographic boundaries (Combating Terrorism Center at West Point 2021, p i). This shift complicates the vulnerability of LGBTQ+ people who may not be able to rely on the enforcement of the protections afforded to them based on national identity. This research is clearly urgent given that in the latest annual EU review of online platforms' compliance with the EU's code, TikTok is the only online platform to have improved on the timely removal of hate speech (Chan 2022).

The growing number of bans on the use of TikTok on government devices across jurisdictions, and a broader call to limit the use of all apps over privacy concerns, speaks to deeper issues over the use of user data, and the necessity for transparency to rebuild trust in institutions, tech corporations, and Western liberal democracy. Central to achieving this aim is documenting the harms perpetuated through the hybrid media ecosystem and through digital platforms, and reductive traditional news media framing in particular, through media monitoring and policy responses based on those findings.

Australia is presenting itself as a paradox. On the one hand, it has been instrumental in introducing a code that regulates big-tech payments to news media outlets for their content. On the other, in a decision that had ramifications for any

Facebook page administrator, the Australian high court ruled in 2021 that media companies could be held liable for allegedly defamatory comments posted to their Facebook pages (Meade 2022). A recent defamation case in Australia has found YouTube liable as a publisher of user-generated content (Barilaro v Google LLC [2022] FCA 650) and reflects the breadth of opportunity to bring about greater transparency and accountability within the hybrid media ecosystem, albeit through a novel application of defamation law that is economically and politically motivated.

At the same time, Australia's Attorney's General are mooting legislation that might allow Australian media companies to avoid liability for defamatory third-party comments on their social media posts (Meade 2022). In an intra-media case, Lachlan Murdoch has brought a defamation case against Australian news media outlet Crikey, over claims that Murdoch illegally conspired with Donald Trump to overturn the 2020 US presidential election result and incite the armed mob that marched on the Capitol in January 2021 to prevent the result from being confirmed (Muller 2022).

The uneven factual accuracy of the OpenAI chatbot, ChatGPT, looks set to further complicate the ambiguities arising from this confluence of ideology, technology and identity formation. The mission of OpenAI, the company that has developed ChatGPT, 'is to ensure that artificial general intelligence benefits all of humanity' (2023, np). This statement is worrisome, and somewhat wearisome, given the altruistic origins of many digital platforms. The range of issues noted in this book that are yet to be addressed by digital platforms, justify this cynicism. Facebook was established in 2004, YouTube in 2005, and Twitter in 2006. So there have roughly been 20 years to consider and address the issues that have arisen from those platforms, yet online hate has increased in recent years.

However, there is also potential in harnessing ethically sourced knowledge through artificial intelligence to further

LGBTQ+ causes. In terms of grey zone operations within the broader geopolitical environment that has seen a shift in focus to espionage as the main threat to sovereignty within Western liberal democracies, at least 19 US states (and many other jurisdictions) have banned or restricted the use of TikTok on government devices over data privacy and national security concerns. These bans are in addition to separate bills to ban TikTok outright, and prohibit its use on government devices pending in the US Congress (Power 2022). At the same time, the European Commission has informed Meta of its preliminary view that the company breached EU anti-trust rules by distorting competition in the markets for online classified ads (European Commission 2022). Russia and its satellites continue to be the main regional threat to LGBTQ+ safety through coercive misinformation and disinformation that conflates sexual politics and Western liberal values to distract from political mismanagement through the imaginary of same-sex attraction as aberrant. Some African nations, such as Ghana and Uganda, continue to represent the extreme end of legislation that seeks to silence and erase LGBTQ+ identity and expression.

Queering it up through digiqueer criminology

Regardless, LGBTQ+ peoples are going to need to continue to keep 'queering it up'. This book has provided food for thought on how to go about this. In doing so it has connected criminological scholarship on representational harms against LGBTQ+ peoples to geopolitical debates on tribalism, nationhood and identity, consumption, and consumerism, procreation, and their relationship with LGBTQ+ identity negotiation.

In this book, the digiqueer citizen has come into sharper focus as an agent to combat representational harms and secure LGBTQ+ recognition and resources. If the aim of the digiqueer citizen is to address inequity against LGBTQ+ individuals and communities, and to effect justice, this book has considered how digital technologies impede and enable that objective.

This research is important given that despite the integration of digital technologies into almost every aspect of daily life, criminological knowledge on the relationship between LGBTQ+ identity formation through digital media technologies and the legal, economic and political value it can generate is limited. This is all the more surprising given the long tradition of social constructionism within criminology, and a focus on symbolic interactionism that seeks to identify patterns of interaction, normative conventions, and dominant definitions of reality formation (Matza 2010). This focus recognizes the constraints on individual and group agency through power relations, and social divisions through labelling (Lemert 1951) – vis-à-vis, stigmatization as a determinant of deviance.

Future research in this area should continue to prioritize the interrelationship between individuals, markets, states and civil society to prevent crime, and in doing so emphasize the significance of freedoms, in this case, LGBTQ+ expression, conduct and relationship rights, to prevent domination (Braithwaite 2022). The continued co-option of same-sex attraction and related gender identity by a range of actors is also in spite of, and a consequence of, the expanding social imagination of homosexuality enhanced by endorsement of same-sex marriage (Hart-Brinson 2016). This expanded social imagination is based on the articulation of sexuality as identity rather than conduct across health and welfare, religion, securitization, markets, nationalism, a sense of belonging, and other identifiers (Richardson 2018). As artificial intelligence and big data continue to shape human relations in unpredictable ways, digiqueer criminology will continue to play a central role in analysis of LGBTQ+ representation and resistance in these technocratic times.

Notes

one Information Warfare in Technocratic Times

[1] The LGBTQ+ initialism used throughout this book encompasses a broad range of sexual orientation and gender identity. This initialism is intended to be inclusive of a range of perspectives and lived experience across these orientations and identities, and at the same time, reflects the limitations of such initialisms in capturing all of those lived experiences. Where alternatives are used, such as LGBT, or LGBTQIA+, those initialisms reflect the samples or perspectives drawn on in the research cited.

three Information Warfare Against Drag Queen Storytime

[1] The reactions to DQS in news media and public discourse analysed in the chapter is based on a ProQuest database search conducted in February 2021. The search was based on the keywords 'drag queen story hour' or 'drag queen storytime' and 'protest'. The DQS terms were selected to reflect the most common terms used for DQS events across jurisdictions and the term 'backlash' was subsequently used in conjunction with 'protest' to narrow the results returned, and in turn, to make data analysis more manageable. The search returned 725 results (441 newspapers, 168 wire feeds, 79 blogs, podcasts and websites, 19 scholarly journals and 18 magazines – full text only results were included, duplicates were excluded), the overwhelming number of which came from the United States. For example, the top 10 results by publication location were mostly from the US, and accounted for 483 individual results out of the 725 results returned in the overall search from four US locations – New York (n=128), San Francisco (n=75), New York City (n=42) and Maine (n=36), in addition to most individual results from the US (n=202). Other locations included Australia, the UK, Canada and Ireland. The focus, however, is on the US, Australia and the UK, given the negative reactions to DQS in those jurisdictions noted in the media.

[2] Trump's embracement of 'anti-LGBTQ hate groups and their agenda of dismantling federal protections and resources for LGBTQ people' was concurrent with his Department of Justice filing 'amicus briefs with the Supreme Court in support of anti-LGBTQ lawsuits, some of which were brought by the anti-LGBTQ hate group Alliance Defending

Freedom' (The Southern Poverty Law Center 2020b, p 13). In October 2019, Trump once again spoke in person to the Values Voter Summit, a gathering of religious-right organizations hosted by the hate group Family Research Council. In May 2019, Trump announced his opposition to the Federal Equality Amendment, which would have added sexual orientation and gender identity to the Civil Rights Act as protected categories regarding employment and housing discrimination (The Southern Poverty Law Center 2020b, p 13). Staffers from organizations that vilify the LGBTQ community were hired by the Trump administration and influenced and wrote its policies. Numerous protections for LGBTQ people were removed through executive action, as when the Interior Department stripped 'sexual orientation' from its anti-discrimination guidelines in 2019 (The Southern Poverty Law Center 2020b, p 13). In addition, the Trump administration consistently claimed that laws and regulations that prohibit discrimination on the basis of sex did not apply to LGBTQ people, and worked to install religious exemptions to civil rights laws (The Southern Poverty Law Center 2020b, p 13). According to a report by Lambda Legal, a third of the more than 50 US circuit court judges nominated by Trump have a 'demonstrated history of anti-LGBTQ bias' (The Southern Poverty Law Center 2020b, p 13). According to the Southern Poverty Law Center, '[m]uch of this growth has taken place among groups at the grassroots level, a surge possibly fuelled by continued anti-LGBTQ sentiment and policy emanating from government officials (The Southern Poverty Law Center 2020b, p 12). They include a network of churches led by Steven Anderson, who once called for President Obama's assassination and is pastor and head of the Faithful Word Baptist Church – a hate group in Arizona – as well as several new chapters of MassResistance, based in Waltham, Massachusetts' (The Southern Poverty Law Center 2020b, p 12).

3   'Their over-all membership appears to have risen as well, despite multiple investigations, indictments, and the arrest of the Proud Boy leader, Enrique Tarrio' (Bernstein and Marritz 2022, p 4).

4   See also Laitner (2018). In Detroit, Michigan in December 2018, Arthur Schaper, who is based in California and is the organizational director for MassResistance, a self-described pro-family civic group (listed by the Southern Poverty Law Center as an anti-LGBTQ hate group, and which has opposed the promotion of gay people in public life), said that his group's local chapter planned to protest the next Drag Queen Story Time in Huntington Woods, which was scheduled for 26 January 2019.

5   See *Christopher et al* v *Lawson et al*, No. H-18-3943 (S.D. Tex.). In Houston, Texas, in January 2019, the US District Court for the Southern District of Texas, Houston Division, dismissed the lawsuit

filed by Chris Sevier and the Warriors for Christ (classified in 2020 by the Southern Poverty Law Center as an anti-LGBTQ hate group, and which has linked LGBT people with pedophilia and zoophilia, and claim that suicide prevention programs aimed at gay youth were created to normalize and 'lure' children into homosexuality) organization that sought to halt the Houston Public Library's sponsorship or hosting of DQS. The court based its decision on the grounds that the court lacked subject-matter jurisdiction because the plaintiffs failed to establish legal standing to sue as they did not show that they suffered an actual 'injury in fact' caused by the defendants' conduct that could be addressed under the law. Even accepting the plaintiffs' allegation that secular humanism could be a religion for Establishment Clause purposes, the plaintiffs failed to allege any facts or basis showing that 'Drag Queen Storytime' is a religious activity. In addition to legal challenges to Houston Public Library's attempts to hold DQS events, the revelation that a registered sex offender had read at a DQS event at Houston Public Library, without having undergone a background check, added to the controversy.

[6] See *Guidry et al* v *Elberson et al*, No. 6:18-cv-01232 (W.D. La.). In Lafayette, Louisiana in January 2019, the US District Court for the Western District of Louisiana, Lafayette Division, dismissed a lawsuit to stop Lafayette Public Library's DQS on the basis that the out-of-state Christian organization bringing the lawsuit had no standing as plaintiffs. The ruling said named plaintiffs Chris Sevier and others failed to show 'dollars-and-cents' injury from the library's DQS as they live out of state and do not pay property taxes. The typical argument brought in such cases is that the LGBTQ community is a faith ideology, and therefore events such as DQS are tantamount to state sponsorship of a religion, and therefore a violation of the First Amendment establishment clause.

[7] Forms of distributive censorship against DQS include the proposed reduction of aid to public libraries that host DQS events, which are underpinned by broader 'libertarian' arguments about tax and state interventionism. As noted by several US public libraries in response to the distributive aspects of debates over DQS events at public libraries, many of these events are not funded directly by libraries but by groups who use public library spaces to hold the events. A further form of distributive discrimination are the prohibitive costs of public and private security to ensure the safety of audiences, staff and presenters, with DQS events postponed and/or cancelled on this basis.

References

Access Now (2021) 'Access Now's public comment to Facebook's Oversight Board case consultation', available from: www.access now.org/cms/assets/uploads/2021/07/Access-Now-FB-OSB-comments-doxing-July-2021.pdf [Accessed 22 July 2022]

Afriat, H., S. Dvir-Gvirsman, K. Tsuriel and L. Ivan (2021) '"This is capitalism. It is not illegal": Users' attitudes toward institutional privacy following the Cambridge Analytica scandal', *The Information Society*, 37(2): 115–27.

Alexander, J. (2020) 'Carlos Maza is back on YouTube and ready to fight', available from: www.theverge.com/tech/2020/1/31/21112 724/carlos-maza-steven-crowder-vox-youtube-harassment-polic ies-breadtube [Accessed 25 January 2022]

Altman, D. (1971/2012) *Homosexual: Oppression and Liberation*, St Lucia: University of Queensland Press.

Amazon Web Services (2022) 'Start moving data and workloads to the cloud', available from: https://pages.awscloud.com/EMEA-Data-Flywheel.html?nc1=f_ls [Accessed 16 March 2022]

Anderson, B. and M.A. Wood (2021) 'Doxxing: A scoping review and typology', in J. Bailey, A. Flynn and N. Henry (eds) *The Emerald International Handbook of Technology-Facilitated Violence and Abuse*, Bingley: Emerald Publishing Limited, pp 205–26.

Anderson, G. and K. Herr (2007) *Encyclopedia of Activism and Social Justice*, Thousand Oaks, CA: SAGE Publications.

Angwin, J., N. Scheiber and A. Tobin (2017) 'Dozens of companies are using Facebook to exclude older workers from job ads', Machine Bias, available from: www.propublica.org/article/faceb ook-ads-age-discrimination-targeting [Accessed 22 October 2021]

Armano, D. (2017) '5 types of activism every brand should prepare for, even if you're not taking sides', *Ad Week*, available from: https:// www.adweek.com/brand-marketing/5-types-of-activism-every-brand-should-preparefor-even-if-youre-not-taking-sides [Accessed 18 July 2017]

Aurora and GiveOut (2022) *Where are the Rainbow Resources? Understanding the Funding Needs of the LGBTIQ+ Community Sector in Australia*, available from: www.rainbowresources.org.au/ [Accessed 18 November 2022]

Australian Communications and Media Authority (2022) 'News media bargaining code', available from: www.acma.gov.au/news-media-bargaining-code [Accessed 26 June 2022]

Australian Human Rights Commission (2021) 'Human rights and technology: Final report', available from: https://humanrights.gov.au/our-work/rights-and-freedoms/publications/human-rights-and-technology-final-report-2021 [Accessed 27 June 2022]

Badgett, M.V.L., K. Waaldijk and Y.v.d.M. Rodgers (2019) 'The relationship between LGBT inclusion and economic development: Macro-level evidence', *World Development*, 120: 1–14.

Baird, B. (2018) 'Twenty-first century LGBTI activism in Australia: The limits of equality', *Australian Historical Studies*, 49(4): 475–92.

Bakir, V., M. Feilzer and A. McStay (2017) 'Introduction to Special Theme Veillance and transparency: A critical examination of mutual watching in the post-Snowden, Big Data era', *Big Data & Society*, 4(1): 1–5.

Ball, M., T. Broderick, J. Ellis, A. Dwyer and N.L. Asquith (2019) 'Introduction: Queer(y)ing justice', *Current Issues in Criminal Justice*, 31(3): 305–10.

Banet-Weiser, S. and K.M. Miltner (2016) '#Masculinity SoFragile: Culture, structure, and networked misogyny', *Feminist Media Studies*, 16(1): 171–4.

Bartosch, J. (2020) 'Drag Queen Story Time is not okay', available from: www.spiked-online.com/2020/03/03/drag-queen-story-time-is-not-okay/ [Accessed 15 March 2021]

Baugher, A.R. and J.A. Gazmararian (2015) 'Masculine gender role stress and violence: A literature review and future directions', *Aggression and Violent Behavior*, 24: 107–12.

Beauchamp, T. (2019) *Going Stealth: Transgender Politics and US Surveillance Practices*, Durham, NC: Duke University Press.

Bell, D. and J. Binnie. (2004) 'Authenticating queer space: Citizenship, urbanism and governance', *Urban Studies,* 41(9): 1807–20.

REFERENCES

Berke, D.S., R.M. Leone, C.S. Hyatt, A. Zeichner and D.J. Parrott (2021) 'Correlates of men's bystander intervention to prevent sexual and relationship violence: The role of masculine discrepancy stress', *Journal of Interpersonal Violence*, 36(21–22): 9877–903.

Berlant, L. (1997) *The Queen of America Goes to Washington City*, Durham, NC: Duke University Press.

Bernstein, A. and I. Marritz (2022) 'Two January 6th defendants and the consolidation of right-wing extremism', *The New Yorker*, available from: www.newyorker.com/news/dispatch/two-janu ary-6th-defendants-and-the-consolidation-of-right-wing-extrem ism [Accessed 26 June 2022]

Betts, D. and J. Bennett (2021) 'An Australian regional response to marriage equality: Newcastle and the hunter', Journal of Homosexuality, 69(11): 1980–2001.

Big Brother Watch (2018) 'Big Brother Watch launches legal challenge to government and Met Police on "dangerously authoritarian" facial recognition cameras', available from: https://bigbrotherwa tch.org.uk/2018/06/big-brother-watch-launches-legal-challe nge-to-government-and-met-police-on-dangerously-authoritar ian-facial-recognition-cameras/ [Accessed 27 June 2022]

Bittner, E. (1970) *Functions of the Police in Modern Society: A Review of Background Factors, Current Practices, and Possible Role Models*, Chevy Chase: National Institute of Mental Health.

Bivens, R. (2017) 'The gender binary will not be deprogrammed: Ten years of coding gender on Facebook', *New Media & Society*, 19(6): 880–98.

Bjork-James, S. (2019) 'Christian nationalism and LGBTQ structural violence in the United States', *Journal of Religion and Violence*, 7(3): 278–302.

Blondeel, K., S. De Vasconcelos, C. García-Moreno, R. Stephenson, M. Temmerman and I. Toskin (2018) 'Violence motivated by perception of sexual orientation and gender identity: A systematic review', *Bulletin of the World Health Organization*, 96(1): 29.

Bogen, K.W., S.L. Williams, D.E. Reidy and L.M. Orchowski (2021) 'We (want to) believe in the best of men: A qualitative analysis of reactions to #Gillette on Twitter', *Psychology of Men & Masculinities*, 22(1): 101.

Bordo, S. (2000) *The Male Body: A New Look at Men in Public and in Private*, New York: Farrar, Straus and Giroux.

Bradford, B. (2014) 'Policing and social identity: Procedural justice, inclusion and cooperation between police and public', *Policing and Society*, 24(1): 22–43.

Bradford, B., J. Milani and J. Jackson (2017) 'Identity, legitimacy and "making sense" of police use of force', *Policing: An International Journal*, 40(3): 614–27.

Bradley, L. (2018) '"I was terrified, and I was humiliated": #MeToo's male accusers, one year later', Vanity Fair, available from: www.vanityfair.com/hollywood/2018/10/metoo-male-accusers-terry-crews-alex-winter-michael-gaston-interview [Accessed 4 August 2022]

Braithwaite, J. (2022) *Macrocriminology and Freedom*, Canberra: ANU Press.

Brooks, V. and J.C. Thompson (2019) 'Dude looks like a lady: Gender deception, consent and ethics', *The Journal of Criminal Law*, 83(4): 258–71.

Brown, E. (2021) 'Sexual assault against boys is a crisis', *Washington Post*, available from: www.washingtonpost.com/magazine/2021/02/22/why-we-dont-talk-about-sexual-violence-against-boys-why-we-should/ [Accessed 4 August 2022]

Browning, K. (2020) 'Twitch suspends Trump's channel for "hateful conduct"', *New York Times*, available from: www.nytimes.com/2020/06/29/technology/twitch-trump.html [Accessed 3 July 2020]

Bullock, C.M. and M. Beckson (2011) 'Male victims of sexual assault: Phenomenology, psychology, physiology', *Journal of the American Academy of Psychiatry and the Law Online*, 39(2): 197–205.

Callaghan, G., R. Feneley, D. Glick, D. McNab, S. Page, S. Thompson et al (2018) *In Pursuit of Truth and Justice: Documenting Gay and Transgender Prejudice Killings in NSW in the Late 20th Century*, Sydney: AIDS Council of NSW.

Cameron, S. and I. McAllister (2019) *The 2019 Australian Federal Election: Results from the Australian Election Study*, Canberra: Australian National University.

Caplan, R. and T. Gillespie (2020) 'Tiered governance and demonetization: The shifting terms of labor and compensation in the platform economy', *Social Media + Society*, 6(2): 2056305120936636.

Cascio, J. (2013) 'Ambiveillance', Jamais Cascio, available from: https://twitter.com/cascio/status/364112024818556928?s=20 [Accessed 19 November 2020]

Castells, M. (2010) *The Power of Identity: Volume 2, with a New Preface*, Wiley Online Library, available from: https://www.wiley.com/en-gb/The+Power+of+Identity%2C+2nd+Edition%2C+with+a+New+Preface-p-9781405196871 [Accessed 10 April 2023]

Cavanagh, N. (2020) 'Parents clash with protesters as drag queen reads to children at library', *Daily Star*, available from: www.dailystar.co.uk/news/world-news/parents-clash-protesters-drag-queen-21353292 [Accessed 18 March 2021]

Center for Countering Digital Hate (2022a) *Digital Hate: Social Media's Role In Amplifying Dangerous Lies About LGBTQ+ People*, London.

Center for Countering Digital Hate (2022b) 'The Musk Bump: Quantifying the rise in hate speech under Elon Musk', available from: https://counterhate.com/blog/the-musk-bump-quantifying-the-rise-in-hate-speech-under-elon-musk/ [Accessed 21 December 2022]

Chadwick, A. (2017) *The Hybrid Media System: Politics and Power*, Oxford: Oxford University Press.

Chan, K. (2022) 'EU review knocks Twitter, others over hate speech removal', *Daily Breeze*, available from: www.dailybreeze.com/2022/11/24/eu-review-knocks-twitter-others-over-hate-speech-removal/ [Accessed 20 December 2022]

Chapman, A. and K. Kelly (2005) 'Australian anti-vilification law: A discussion of the public/private divide and the work relations context', *Sydney Law Review*, 27: 203–36.

Chesney, L. (2017) 'LGBT buying power closer to one trillion dollars', *Western New York Gay and Lesbian Yellow Pages*, available from: http://wnygaypages.com/lgbt-buying-power/ [Accessed 23 February 2023]

Chomsky, N. and E. Herman (1988) *Manufacturing Consent*, New York: Pantheon.

Cockburn, P. (2020) 'Sydney Mardi Gras votes to keep NSW Police and Liberal Party at future parades', available from: www.abc.net. au/news/2020-12-05/mardi-gras-votes-to-keep-nsw-police-in-parade/12954180 [Accessed 9 December 2020]

Colbran, M.P. (2022) *Crime and Investigative Reporting in the UK*, Bristol: Bristol University Press.

Combating Terrorism Center at West Point (2021) *CTC Sentinel*, July/August, 14(6).

Commonwealth of Australia (2017) *Royal Commission into Institutional Responses to Child Sexual Abuse: Final Report, Volume 1*, Canberra.

Commonwealth of Australia (2022) 'Inquiry into social media and online safety', available from: www.aph.gov.au/Parliamentary_B usiness/Committees/House/Social_Media_and_Online_Safety/ SocialMediaandSafety [Accessed 21 January 2022]

Corey, A.M. (2019) 'Love is love is love is love: From flaktivism to consumer activism in LGBTQ+ communities', *Queer Studies in Media & Pop Culture*, 4: 117–37.

Cosentino, G. (2020) *Social Media and the Post-Truth World Order*, Cham: Springer.

Crampton, J.W. (2019) 'Platform biometrics', *Surveillance & Society*, 17(1/2): 54–62.

Crown Prosecution Service (2017) 'Hate crime', available from: www. cps.gov.uk/crime-info/hate-crime [Accessed 20 May 2021]

d'Emilio, J. (1983/2007) *Capitalism and Gay Identity*, London: Routledge.

Dame, A. (2016) 'Making a name for yourself: Tagging as transgender ontological practice on Tumblr', *Critical Studies in Media Communication*, 33(1): 23–37.

Donnelly-Drummond, A. (2021) 'LGBTQs and LAW'S violence within a heteronormative landscape', *Frontiers in Sociology*, 6, DOI: 10.3389/fsoc.2021.564028.

Drag Queen Story Hour (2020) 'Drag Queen Story Hour: About', available from: www.dragqueenstoryhour.org/about/ [Accessed 18 Feburary 2020]

REFERENCES

Duggan, L. (2002) 'The new homonormativity: The sexual politics of neoliberalism', in R. Castronovo and D.D. Nelson (eds) *Materializing Democracy: Toward a Revitalized Cultural Politics*, New York: Duke University Press, pp 175–94.

Duncan, S.G., G. Aguilar, C.G. Jensen and B.M. Magnusson (2019) 'Survey of heteronormative attitudes and tolerance toward gender non-conformity in Mountain West undergraduate students', *Frontiers in Psychology*, 10: 793.

Duncanson, K. (2013) *Community Beliefs and Misconceptions about Male Sexual Assault*, Melbourne: Australian Institute of Family Studies.

Durkin, E. (2019) 'New Gillette ad shows father helping transgender son to shave', *The Guardian*, available from: www.theguardian.com/world/2019/may/28/gillette-ad-shaving-transgender-son-samson-bonkeabanut-brown [Accessed 4 August 2022]

Dwoskin, E. and C. Timberg (2021) 'Misinformation dropped dramatically the week after Twitter banned Trump', *Washington Post*, available from: www.washingtonpost.com/technology/2021/01/16/misinformation-trump-twitter/ [Accessed 17 January 2021]

Dwyer, A., M. Ball and T. Crofts (eds) (2016) *Queering Criminology*, Basingstoke: Palgrave Macmillan.

Eaton, R., R. Odermatt and G. Ringler (2021) 'The case for intermediaries: Navigating Australia's LGBTIQ not-for-profit landscape', available at: https://www.oliverwyman.com/our-culture/society/social-impact/the-case-for-intermediaries.html [Accessed 24 February 2023]

Eberstadt, M. (2019) 'The lure of androgyny', *Commentary Magazine*, 148(3 March): 28–31.

Ecker, S., E.D.b. Riggle, S.S. Rostosky and J.M. Byrnes (2019) 'Impact of the Australian marriage equality postal survey and debate on psychological distress among lesbian, gay, bisexual, transgender, intersex and queer/questioning people and allies', *Australian Journal of Psychology*, 71(3): 285–95.

Economist, The (2022) 'Britain's Online Safety Bill could change the face of the internet', *The Economist*, available from: www.economist.com/britain/2022/05/25/britains-online-safety-billcould-change-the-face-of-the-internet [Accessed 26 June 2022]

Edwards, G.S. and S. Rushin (2018) 'The effect of President Trump's election on hate crimes', available from: https://ssrn.com/abstract=3102652 [Accessed 18 November 2022]

Eisend, M. and E. Hermann (2019) 'Consumer responses to homosexual imagery in advertising: A meta-analysis', *Journal of Advertising*, 48(4): 380–400.

Electronic Frontier Foundation (2023) 'About EFF', available from: https://www.eff.org/about [Accessed 16 February 2023]

Ellis, J.R. (2021) *Policing Legitimacy: Social Media, Scandal and Sexual Citizenship*, Cham: Springer.

Ellis, J.R. (2022) 'A fairy tale gone wrong: Social media, recursive hate and the politicisation of Drag Queen Storytime', *The Journal of Criminal Law*, 86(2): 94–108, https://doi.org/10.1177/00220183221086455

Ellis, J.R. (2023) 'Social media, police excessive force and the limits of outrage: Evaluating models of police scandal', *Criminology and Criminal Justice*, 23(1): 117–134, https://doi.org/10.1177/17488958211017384

Elphick, L. (2017) 'Sexual orientation and "gay wedding cake" cases under Australian anti-discrimination legislation: A fuller approach to religious exemptions', *The Adelaide Law Review*, 38(1): 149–93.

eSafety Commissioner (2021) *Protecting LGBTIQ+ Voices Online: Resource Development Research*, available from: www.esafety.gov.au/research/protecting-lgbtiq-voices-online [Accessed 18 November 2022]

Esmark, A. (2020) *The New Technocracy*, Bristol: Policy Press.

European Centre of Excellence for Countering Hybrid Threats (2022) 'Hybrid threats as a concept', available from: www.hybridcoe.fi/hybrid-threats-as-a-phenomenon/ [Accessed 26 June 2022]

REFERENCES

European Commission (2020) 'Union of Equality: The Commission presents its first-ever strategy on LGBTIQ equality in the EU', press release, available from: https://ec.europa.eu/commission/presscorner/detail/en/ip_20_2068 [Accessed 26 July 2022]

European Commission (2022) 'The Digital Services Act package', available from: https://digital-strategy.ec.europa.eu/en/policies/digital-services-act-package [Accessed 9 January 2023]

Fabiani, A. (2021) 'Twitch sues users over "hate raids" targeted at black and LGBTQ streamers', *Screenshot*, available from: https://screenshot-media.com/about/ [Accessed 26 July 2022]

Farmer, P. (2004) 'An anthropology of structural violence', *Current Anthropology*, 45(3): 305–25.

Fasoli, F., P. Hegarty and D.M. Frost (2021) 'Stigmatization of "gay-sounding" voices: The role of heterosexual, lesbian, and gay individuals' essentialist beliefs', *British Journal of Social Psychology*, 60(3): 826–50.

Feeley, M. and J. Simon (1994) 'Actuarial justice: The emerging new criminal law', *The Futures of Criminology*, 173: 174.

Filice, E., A. Raffoul, S.B. Meyer and E. Neiterman (2020) 'Impact of social media on body image perceptions and bodily practices among gay, bisexual, and other men who have sex with men: A critical review of the literature and extension of theory', *Sex Roles*, 82(7): 387–410.

Flores, A.R. (2021) 'Social acceptance of LGBTI people in 175 countries and locations', UCLA Williams Institute School of Law, available from: https://williamsinstitute.law.ucla.edu/publications/global-acceptance-index-lgbt/ [Accessed 25 August 2022]

Foltz, R. (2022) 'Homophobia as a wartime marketing tool: Some Russians fear the West will make them gay', *The Conversation*, available from: https://theconversation.com/homophobia-as-a-wartime-marketing-tool-some-russians-fear-the-west-will-make-them-gay-192826 [Accessed 8 December 2022]

Foucault, M. (1981) *The History of Sexuality, Vol. 1: An Introduction*, Harmondsworth: Penguin.

Foucault, M. and F. Ewald (2003) *'Society Must Be Defended': Lectures at the Collège de France, 1975–1976*, New York: Picador.

Funke, D. (2022) 'Drag Queen Story Hour head not arrested for child porn', *Agence France-Presse Fact Check*, available from: https://factcheck.afp.com/doc.afp.com.32CY2TG [Accessed 24 June 2022]

Galtung, J. (1969) 'Violence, peace, and peace research', *Journal of Peace Research*, 6(3): 167–91.

Gan, N. and Y. Xiong. (2021) 'WeChat deletes dozens of university LGBT accounts in China', *CNN Business*, available from: https://edition.cnn.com/2021/07/07/business/china-lgbt-wechat-censorship-intl-hnk/index.html [Accessed 23 January 2023]

Gandy, O.H. (1993) 'Toward a political economy of personal information', *Critical Studies in Mass Communication*, 10(1): 70–97.

Garland, D. (2013) 'Penality and the penal state', *Criminology*, 51(3): 475–517.

Gates, K.A. (2011) *Our Biometric Future*, New York: New York University Press.

Gen, S. and A.C. Wright (2013) 'Policy advocacy organizations: A framework linking theory and practice', *Journal of Policy Practice*, 12(3): 163–93.

Ghaziani, A. (2008) *The Dividends of Dissent: How Conflict and Culture Work in Lesbian and Gay Marches on*, Chicago, IL: University of Chicago Press.

Gingerich, M. (2022) 'Tim Pool exemplifies YouTube's failure to moderate anti-LGTBQ hate speech', *Media Matters for America*, available from: www.mediamatters.org/tim-pool/tim-pool-exemplifies-youtubes-failure-moderate-anti-lgtbq-hate-speech [Accessed 3 August 2022]

GLAAD and Procter & Gamble (2019) 'LGBTQ inclusion in advertising and media: Executive summary', available from: www.glaad.org/sites/default/files/P%26G_AdvertisingResearch.pdf [Accessed 18 November 2022]

Global Project Against Hate and Extremism (2022a) *Conversion Therapy Online: The Ecosystem*, available from: https://globalextremism.org/reports/conversion-therapy-online-the-ecosystem/ [Accessed 18 November 2022]

Global Project against Hate and Extremism (2022b) *Conversion Therapy Online: The Players*, available from: https://globalex tremism.org/reports/conversion-therapy-online-the-players/ [Accessed 18 November 2022]

Goldberg, M. (2019) 'Leave Drag Queen Story Hour alone!', *The New York Times*, available from: www.nytimes.com/2019/06/07/opinion/conservatives-culture-trump.html [Accessed 7 March 2021]

Goodnight, B. (2016) 'Anonymity and anti-gay aggression in an online sample: The effect of an audience on gender role enforcement', PhD thesis, Georgia State University.

Government of India (2021) 'Government notifies Information Technology (Intermediary Guidelines and Digital Media Ethics Code) Rules 2021', available from: https://pib.gov.in/PressRelese Detailm.aspx?PRID=1700749 [Accessed 26 June 2022]

Gray, M.L. (2010) 'From websites to Wal-Mart: Youth, identity work, and the queering of boundary publics in small town, USA', in C. Pullen and M. Cooper (eds) *LGBT Identity and Online New Media*, New York: Routledge, pp 302–12.

Grayson, N. (2021) 'Twitch hate raids are more than just a Twitch problem, and they're only getting worse', *The Washington Post*, available from: www.washingtonpost.com/video-games/2021/08/25/twitch-hate-raids-streamers-discord-cybersecurity/ [Accessed 26 July 2022]

Greene, A. (2020) 'Right-wing extremists using Islamic State tactics to recruit, ASIO warns, amid spike in surveillance', *ABC News*, available from: www.abc.net.au/news/2020-09-22/right-wing-extremists-asio-islamic-state-tactics/12690002 [Accessed 29 October 2020]

Greer, C. and E. McLaughlin. (2017) 'Theorizing institutional scandal and the regulatory state', *Theoretical Criminology*, 21(2): 112–32.

Gregory, S. (2019) 'Cameras everywhere revisited: How digital technologies and social media aid and inhibit human rights documentation and advocacy', *Journal of Human Rights Practice*, 11(2): 373–92.

Hale, S.E. and T. Ojeda (2018) 'Acceptable femininity? Gay male misogyny and the policing of queer femininities', *European Journal of Women's Studies*, 25(3): 310–24.

Hall, S. (ed) (1997) *Representation: Cultural Representations and Signifying Practices*, London: SAGE.

Hao, K. (2020) 'We read the paper that forced Timnit Gebru out of Google: Here's what it says', *MIT Technology Review*, available from: https://www.technologyreview.com/2020/12/04/1013 294/google-ai-ethics-research-paper-forced-out-timnit-gebru/ [Accessed 24 July 2022]

Harrison, B.F. and M.R. Michelson (2017) *Listen, We Need to Talk: How to Change Attitudes About LGBT Rights*, Oxford: Oxford University Press.

Hart-Brinson, P. (2016) 'The social imagination of homosexuality and the rise of same-sex marriage in the United States', *Socius*, 2: 2378023116630555

Hayward, L. (2020) 'Information warfare, accelerated warfare and the human endeavour', *Australian Army Journal*, 16(1): 33–46.

Hern, A. (2019) 'TikTok's local moderation guidelines ban pro-LGBT content', *The Guardian*, available from: www.theguardian.com/technology/2019/sep/26/tiktoks-local-moderation-guideli nes-ban-pro-lgbt-content [Accessed 2 July 2022]

Hern, A. (2020) 'Twitter hides Donald Trump tweet for "glorifying violence"', *The Guardian*, available from: www.theguardian.com/technology/2020/may/29/twitter-hides-donald-trump-tweet-glorifying-violence [Accessed 3 July 2020]

Hesse, M. (2022) 'Fans of Florida's "Don't Say Gay" bill have a new favorite word: "Grooming"', *Washington Post*, available from: www.washingtonpost.com/lifestyle/2022/03/12/florida-dont-say-gay-bill/ [Accessed 26 June 2022]

House of Lords and House of Commons (2021) *Draft Online Safety Bill: Report of Session 2021–22*.

Howcroft, E. and G. Chavez-Dreyfuss (2021) 'Meet the trans teen whose crypto artwork has earned him nearly $50 million', *Reuters*, available from: www.reuters.com/technology/crypto-art-about-gender-transition-fetches-216-mln-christies-2021-06-30/ [Accessed 6 July 2022]

Hudson-Sharp, N. and H. Metcalf (2016) *Inequality Among Lesbian, Gay Bisexual and Transgender Groups in the UK: A Review of Evidence*, London: National Institute of Economic and Social Research.

Human Rights Campaign (2022) '200+ major U.S. companies oppose anti-LGBTQ+ state legislation', available from: www.hrc.org/press-releases/200-major-u-s-companies-oppose-anti-lgbtq-state-legislation [Accessed 26 July 2022]

Human Rights Campaign (2023) 'Human rights campaign slams Governor Lee for signing Anti-Drag bill and Gender Affirming Care Ban into Law: TN becomes first state to criminalize drag', available from: https://www.hrc.org/press-releases/human-rights-campaign-slams-governor-lee-for-signing-anti-drag-bill-and-gender-affirming-care-ban-into-law-tn-becomes-first-state-to-criminalize-drag [Accessed 14 March 2023]

ILGA World (2020a) *Curbing Deception: A World Survey on Legal Regulation of So-Called 'Conversion Therapies'*, Geneva: ILGA World.

ILGA World (2020b) *State-Sponsored Homophobia 2020: Global Legislation Overview Update*, Geneva: ILGA World.

Inglehart, R. (1981) 'Post-materialism in an environment of insecurity', *The American Political Science Review*, 75(4), 880–900.

Insikt Group (2020) *Online Surveillance, Censorship, and Discrimination for LGBTQIA+ Community Worldwide*, Boston: Recorded Future.

Insikt Group (2021) *Pride and Prejudice in Shifting Landscape of LGBTQIA+ Laws Worldwide*, Boston: Recorded Future.

Insikt Group (2022) *Threat Analysis: Russia's War Against Ukraine: Effects on the Ukrainian LGBTQIA+ Community*, Boston: Recorded Future.

Jansson, A. (2015) 'Interveillance: A new culture of recognition and mediatization', *Media and Communication*, 3(3): 81–90.

Jones, J. (2022) 'LGBT identification in U.S. ticks up to 7.1%', *Gallup*, available from: https://news.gallup.com/poll/389792/lgbt-identification-ticks-up.aspx [Accessed 12 January 2023]

Jones, C., V. Trott and S. Wright (2020) 'Sluts and soyboys: MGTOW and the production of misogynistic online harassment', *New Media & Society*, 22(10): 1903–21.

Kafer, G. and D. Grinberg (2019) 'Queer surveillance', *Surveillance & Society,* 17(5): 592–601.

Karizat, N., D. Delmonaco, M. Eslami and N. Andalibi (2021) 'Algorithmic folk theories and identity: How TikTok users co-produce knowledge of identity and engage in algorithmic resistance', *Proceedings of the ACM on Human-Computer Interaction,* 5(CSCW2): Article 305.

Keck, T.M. (2009) 'Beyond backlash: Assessing the impact of judicial decisions on LGBT rights', *Law & Society Review,* 43(1): 151–186.

Kiat, L.S. (nd) 'Machines gone wrong', available from: https://machinesgonewrong.com/bias_i/#two-types-of-harms [Accessed 1 July 2022]

Kiss, L., M. Quinlan-Davidson, L. Pasquero, P.O. Tejero, C. Hogg, J. Theis et al (2020) 'Male and LGBT survivors of sexual violence in conflict situations: A realist review of health interventions in low-and middle-income countries', *Conflict and Health,* 14(1): 11.

Kitzie, V. (2019) '"That looks like me or something I can do": Affordances and constraints in the online identity work of US LGBTQ+ millennials', *Journal of the Association for Information Science and Technology,* 70(12): 1340–51.

Laitner, B. (2018) 'Drag Queen Story Hour to continue', *Detroit Free Press,* available from: www.proquest.com/docview/2158159861?accountid=10499&forcedol=true&parentSessionId=OuJneNhxhf5J86Zy4W9b8X0%2ByaZhHjy8MffRtJq5c6o%3D [Accessed 18 March 2021]

Lauder, S. (2015) 'The Capability: Government's national facial recognition plan raises privacy concerns', *ABC News,* available from: www.abc.net.au/news/2015-12-17/governments-facial-recognition-system-sparks-privacy-concerns/7035980 [Accessed 12 January 2023]

Lauer, D. (2021) 'Facebook's ethical failures are not accidental: They are part of the business model', *AI and Ethics,* 1(4): 395–403.

Lee, M., J. Ellis, C. Keel, J. Jackson and R. Wickes (2022) 'When law and order politics fail: Identifying protective factors that limit the politics of fear', *British Journal of Criminology,* 62(5): 1270–88.

Lemert, E.M. (1951) *Social Pathology: A Systematic Approach to The theory of Sociopathic Behavior*, New York: McGraw-Hill.

Lewis, C. (2022) 'Alex Jones proves there are limits on expression but not on the grift', *Crikey*, available from: www.crikey.com.au/2022/10/13/alex-jones-payment-sandy-hook-verdict-grift/ [Accessed 13 October]

Lewis, R. (2018) *Alternative Influence: Broadcasting the Reactionary Right on YouTube*, New York: Data & Society.

LGBT Tech (2021) 'Research', available from: www.lgbttech.org/ [Accessed 20 October 2021]

Lih Yi, B. (2020) 'Japan firms back same-sex partnership certificate campaign in gay rights push', *Reuters*, available from: www.reuters.com/article/us-japan-lgbt-rights-trfn-idUSKBN22B1HZ [Accessed 6 July 2022]

Lin, J.A. (2021) *Gay Bar: Why We Went Out*, London: Hachette.

Lindtner, S., J. Chen, G.R. Hayes and P. Dourish (2011) 'Towards a framework of publics: Re-encountering media sharing and its user', *ACM Transactions on Computer-Human Interaction* 18(2): Article 5.

Littman, L. (2021) 'Individuals treated for gender dysphoria with medical and/or surgical transition who subsequently detransitioned: A survey of 100 detransitioners', *Archives of Sexual Behavior*, 50(8): 3353–69.

Loader, I. and R. Sparks (2013) 'Unfinished business: Legitimacy, crime control and democratic politics', in J. Tankebe and A. Liebling (eds) *Legitimacy and Criminal Justice: An International Exploration*, Oxford: Oxford University Press, pp 105–26.

Lyon, D. (2003) *Surveillance as Social Sorting: Privacy, Risk, and Digital Discrimination*, Oxford: Psychology Press.

Madrigal-Borloz, V. (2019) *Data Collection and Management as a Means to Create Heightened Awareness of Violence and Discrimination Based on Sexual Orientation and Gender Identity*, UNHCR Thematic Report A/HRC/41/45.

Madrigal–Borloz, V. (2021) 'The price that is paid: Violence and discrimination based on sexual orientation and gender identity and poverty', in M.F. Davis, M. Kjaerum and A. Lyons (eds) *Research Handbook on Human Rights and Poverty*, Cheltenham: Edward Elgar Publishing.

Magnet, S.A. (2011) *When Biometrics Fail: Gender, Race, and the Technology of Identity*, Durham, NC: Duke University Press.

Marsh, I. and L. Galbraith (1995) 'The political impact of the Sydney Gay and Lesbian Mardi Gras', *Australian Journal of Political Science*, 30(2): 300–20.

Mason, G. (2008) 'Hate crime', in T. Anthony and C. Cuneen (eds) *The Critical Criminology Companion*, Leichhardt: Hawkins Press, pp 180–90.

Mason, G. (2014) 'The hate threshold: Emotion, causation and difference in the construction of prejudice-motivated crime', *Social & Legal Studies: An International Journal*, 23(3): 293–314.

Mason, M. (2022) 'Barilaro's defamation win signals new world for digital platforms', available from: https://www.afr.com/compan ies/media-and-marketing/barilaro-s-defamation-win-signals-new-world-for-digital-platforms-20220607-p5arr3 [Accessed 26 June 2022]

Mason, G. and N. Czapski (2017) 'Regulating cyber-racism', *Melbourne University Law Review*, 41: 284.

Mason, G. and S. Tomsen (eds) (1997) *Homophobic Violence*, Leichhardt: Hawkins Press.

Matza, D. (2010) *Becoming Deviant*, New York: Routledge.

McInroy, L.B., I. Zapcic and O. W. Beer (2022) 'Online fandom communities as networked counterpublics: LGBTQ+ youths' perceptions of representation and community climate', *Convergence*, 28(3): 629–47.

Meade, A. (2021) 'Sky News Australia banned from YouTube for seven days over Covid misinformation', *The Guardian*, available from: www.theguardian.com/media/2021/aug/01/sky-news-australia-banned-from-youtube-for-seven-days-over-covid-mis information [Accessed 19 Jun 2022]

Meade, A. (2022) 'Defamation reforms: Australian media may not be liable for Facebook comments in future', *The Guardian*, available from: https://www.theguardian.com/media/2022/dec/14/defamation-reforms-australian-media-may-not-be-liable-for-facebook-comments-in-future [Accessed 20 December 2022]

Mehrabi, N., P. Zhou, F. Morstatter, J. Pujara, X. Ren and A. Galstyan (2021) 'Lawyers are dishonest? Quantifying representational harms in commonsense knowledge resources', arXiv:2103.11320.

Miles-Johnson, T. (2016) 'Perceptions of group value: How Australian transgender people view policing', *Policing and Society*, 26(6): 605–26.

Milfeld, T. and D.J. Flint (2021) 'When brands take a stand: The nature of consumers' polarized reactions to social narrative videos', *Journal of Product & Brand Management*, 30(4): 532–48.

Mitchell, K.J., M.L. Ybarra, J.D. Korchmaros and J.G. Kosciw (2014) 'Accessing sexual health information online: Use, motivations and consequences for youth with different sexual orientations', *Health Education Research*, 29(1): 147–157.

Möllers, N., D.M. Wood and D. Lyon (2019) 'Surveillance capitalism: An interview with Shoshana Zuboff', *Surveillance & Society*, 17(1/2): 257–66.

Morgan, H., A. O'Donovan, R. Almeida, A. Lin and Y. Perry. (2020) 'The role of the avatar in gaming for trans and gender diverse young people', *International Journal Environmental Research and Public Health*, 17(22): 8617.

Mouzos, J. and S. Thompson (2000) 'Gay-hate related homicides: An overview of major findings in New South Wales', *Trends & Issues in Crime and Criminal Justice*, 155, Canberra: Australian Institute of Criminology.

Muller, D. (2022) 'Murdoch v Crikey highlights how Australia's defamation laws protect the rich and powerful', *The Conversation*, available from: https://theconversation.com/murdoch-v-crikey-highlights-how-australias-defamation-laws-protect-the-rich-and-powerful-189228 [Accessed 26 August 2022]

Mundt, M., K. Ross and C.M. Burnett (2018) 'Scaling social movements through social media: The case of Black Lives Matter', *Social Media + Society*, 4(4): 2056305118807911.

Navar-Gill, A. and M. Stanfill (2018) '"We shouldn't have to trend to make you listen": Queer fan hashtag campaigns as production interventions', *Journal of Film and Video*, 70(3–4): 85–100.

Nebeling Petersen, M. and K. Hvidtfeldt (2020) '"The best men can be": New configurations of masculinity in the Gillette ad "We believe"', *Women, Gender & Research*, 29(1): 6–18.

Nett, D. (2019) 'Is YouTube doing enough to stop harassment of LGBTQ content creators?', *NPR*, available from: www.npr.org/2019/06/08/730608664/is-youtube-doing-enough-to-stop-harassment-of-lgbtq-content-creators [Accessed 19 August]

Newbery, E. (2021) 'How crypto could help LGBTQ communities', *The Ascent*, available from: www.fool.com/the-ascent/cryptocurrency/articles/how-crypto-could-help-lgbtq-communities/ [Accessed 5 July 2022]

Newman, N., R. Fletcher, A. Kalogeropoulos and R. Nielsen (2019) *Reuters Institute Digital News Report 2019*, Oxford: Reuters Institute, University of Oxford.

Newman, N., R. Fletcher, A. Schulz, S. Andi and R. Nielsen (2020) *Reuters Institute Digital News Report 2020*, Oxford: Reuters Institute, University of Oxford.

Nicholas, L. and C. Agius (2018) *The Persistence of Global Masculinism*, Cham: Springer.

Nielsen (2021) *Proud & Present LGBTQ Audiences & Content Take Center Stage*, Nielsen Diverse Intelligence Series, New York City.

Nussbaum, M.C. (2001) *Women and Human Development: The Capabilities Approach, Volume 3*, Cambridge: Cambridge University Press.

Oakenfull, G. and T. Greenlee. (2004) 'The three rules of crossing over from gay media to mainstream media advertising: Lesbians, lesbians, lesbians', *Journal of Business Research*, 57(11): 1276–85.

REFERENCES

Office of the Australian Information Commissioner (2021) 'Clearview AI breached Australians' privacy', available from: https://www.oaic.gov.au/updates/news-and-media/clearview-ai-breached-australians-privacy#:~:text=Australian%20Information%20Commissioner%20and%20Privacy,through%20a%20facial%20recognition%20tool [Accessed 22 December 2022]

OutRight Action International (2018) *The Global State of LGBTIQ Organizing*, New York: OutRight Action International.

OutRight Action International (2021) 'OutRight Now: October 2021 Newsletter', available from: https://outrightinternational.org/content/outright-now-october-2021-newsletter [Accessed 27 January 2022]

OutRight Action International (2022) *WE DESERVE PROTECTION: Anti-LGBTIQ Legislation and Violence in Ghana*, New York: OutRight International.

Papadopoulos, D. (2003) 'The ordinary superstition of subjectivity: Liberalism and technostructural violence', *Theory & Psychology*, 13(1): 73–93.

Park, A. (2016) *A Development Agenda for Sexual and Gender Minorities*, Los Angeles, CA: Williams Institute, UCLA School of Law.

Parrott, D.J. (2009) 'Aggression toward gay men as gender role enforcement: Effects of male role norms, sexual prejudice, and masculine gender role stress', *Journal of Personality*, 77(4): 1137–66.

Phillips, D.J. and C. Cunningham (2007) 'Queering surveillance research', in K. O'Riordan and D. Phillips (eds) *Queer Online: Media Technology and Sexuality*, Lausanne: Peter Lang, pp 31–44.

Piza, E.L., J. Szkola and K.-L. Blount-Hill (2021) 'How can embedded criminologists, police pracademics, and crime analysts help increase police-led program evaluations? A survey of authors cited in the evidence-based policing matrix', *Policing: A Journal of Policy and Practice*, 15(2): 1217–31.

Powell, A., G. Stratton and R. Cameron (2018) *Digital Criminology: Crime and Justice in Digital Society*, New York: Routledge.

Puar, J. (2013) 'Rethinking homonationalism', *International Journal of Middle East Studies*, 45(2): 336–39.

Puar, J.K. (2007) *Terrorist Assemblages: Homonationalism in Queer Times*, Durham, NC: Duke University Press.

Queenly NFT, The (2021) 'The Queenly NFT: Home', available from: www.queenlynft.com/ [Accessed 21 November 2022]

Rauchberg, J.S. (2022) '#Shadowbanned: Queer, Trans, and Disabled creator responses to algorithmic oppression on TikTok', in P. Palin (ed) *LGBTQ Digital Cultures: A Global Perspective,* New York: Routledge, pp 196–209.

Renninger, B.J. (2015) '"Where I can be myself ... where I can speak my mind": Networked counterpublics in a polymedia environment', *New Media & Society*, 17(9): 1513–29.

Rev.com (2021) 'Facebook whistleblower Frances Haugen testifies on children and social media use: Full senate hearing transcript', available from: https://www.rev.com/blog/transcripts/faceb ook-whistleblower-frances-haugen-testifies-on-children-social-media-use-full-senate-hearing-transcript [Accessed 6 July 2022]

Richardson, D. (2017) 'Rethinking sexual citizenship', *Sociology*, 51(2): 208–24.

Richardson, D. (2018) *Sexuality and Citizenship*, Cambridge: Polity.

Richardson, D. and V. Robinson (2020) *Introducing Gender and Women's Studies*, New York: Red Globe Press.

Robards, B., P. Byron and S. D'Souza (2021) 'LGBTQ+ communities and digital media', in D.A. Rohlinger and S. Sobieraj (eds) *The Oxford Handbook of Digital Media Sociology*, Oxford: Oxford University Press, pp 339–61.

Roberts, M. (2022) 'Western Australian teacher forced to quit job after being outed by students on TikTok', available from: https://junkee.com/tiktok-gay-western-australia/336122 [Accessed 21 July 2022]

Robinson, S. (2008) *Homophobia: An Australian History*, Alexandria: Federation Press.

Robinson, S. and A. Greenwich (2018) *Yes Yes Yes: Australia's Journey to Marriage Equality*, Sydney: NewSouth Books.

REFERENCES

Rollè, L., G. Giardina, A.M. Caldarera, E. Gerino and P. Brustia (2018) 'When intimate partner violence meets same sex couples: A review of same sex intimate partner violence', *Frontiers in Psychology*, 9: 1506.

Roose, K. (2020) 'Reddit's C.E.O. on why he banned "The_Donald" Subreddit', *The New York Times*, available from: www.nytimes.com/2020/06/30/us/politics/reddit-bans-steve-huffman.html?searchResultPosition=1 [Accessed 3 July 2020]

Ross, C.J. (2017) 'Assaultive words and constitutional norms', *Journal of Legal Education*, 66(4): 739–76.

Rothkopf, J. (2020) 'Deepfake technology enters the documentary world', *The New York Times*, available from: https://www.nytimes.com/2020/07/01/movies/deepfakes-documentary-welcome-to-chechnya.html [Accessed 22 January 2023]

Russell, E.K. (2020) *Queer Histories and the Politics of Policing*, Oxford: Routledge.

Ryan, F., A. Fritz and D. Impiombato (2020) *TikTok and WeChat: Curating and Controlling Global Information Flows*, Canberra: Australian Strategic Policy Institute.

Sabatier, P.A. (1999) 'The need for better theories', in P.A. Sabatier (ed) *Theories of the Policy Process*, Boulder, CO: Westview Press, pp 3–18.

Sable, M.R., F. Danis, D.L. Mauzy and S.K. Gallagher (2006) 'Barriers to reporting sexual assault for women and men: Perspectives of college students', *Journal of American College Health*, 55(3): 157–62.

salty.com (2022) 'Shadowbanning is a thing – and it's hurting trans and disabled advocates', available from: https://saltyworld.net/shadowbanning-is-a-thing-and-its-hurting-trans-and-disabled-advocates/ [Accessed 29 November 2022]

Santoscoy, C. (2012) 'Time Warner to pay gay couple's tax on benefits', *On Top Magazine*, available from: www.ontopmag.com/about [Accessed 3 August 2022]

Schermele, Z. (2022) 'Texas GOP looks to restrict transgender health care and drag shows', *CBS News*, available from: www.nbcnews. com/nbc-out/out-politics-and-policy/texas-gop-looks-restr ict-transgender-health-care-drag-shows-rcna57346 [Accessed 7 December 2022]

Schudson, Z. and S. van Anders (2019) '"You have to coin new things": Sexual and gender identity discourses in asexual, queer, and/or trans young people's networked counterpublics', *Psychology & Sexuality*, 10(4): 354–68.

Scott, S. (2015) *Negotiating Identity: Symbolic Interactionist Approaches to Social Identity*, Cambridge: Polity Press.

Sedgwick, E.K. (2015) *Between Men: English Literature and Male Homosocial Desire*, New York: Columbia University Press.

Sen, A. (1999) *Development as Freedom*, Oxford: Oxford University Press.

Sengupta, K. (2020) 'Violent right-wing extremism is a "major threat" in the UK, MI5 boss says', *Independent*, available from: www. independent.co.uk/news/uk/home-news/right-wing-extrem ism-terrorism-violence-uk-mi5-ken-mccallum-b1039501.html [Accessed 15 March 2021]

Shapiro, S. (2022) 'DeSantis's attack on Disney will likely fail – and that's probably OK with him', The Hill available from: https:// thehill.com/opinion/campaign/3473539-desantiss-attack-on-disney-will-likely-fail-and-thats-probably-ok-with-him/ [Accessed 7 February 2023]

Shephard, N. (2016) 'Big data and sexual surveillance', Issues Paper, Association for Progressive Communications, Melville, South Africa, available from: https://www.apc.org/en/pubs/big-data-and-sexual-surveillance [Accessed 20 November 2022]

Shrum, H. (2021) 'Author pulls bill to punish schools, libraries for distributing "harmful material"', *Kokomo Tribune*, available from: www.kokomotribune.com/news/local_news/author-pulls-bill-to-punish-schools-libraries-for-distributing-harmful-mater ial/article_ee435a88-7786-11eb-a356-3b3d0ec357b3.html [Accessed 27 June 2022]

Simms, D. (2022) 'How the world's largest collection of LGBTQ-inspired NFT art is raising money for good causes', *Robb Report*, available from: https://robbreport.com/lifestyle/news/pride-icons-nft-artworks-1234681588/ [Accessed 6 July 2022]

Slagboom, M.N., M.R. Crone and R. Reis (2020) 'Exploring syndemic vulnerability across generations: A case study of a former fishing village in the Netherlands', *Social Science & Medicine*, 295: 113122.

Social Talks, The (2022) 'Meta reworks its doxxing policies and puts an end to a dangerous loophole', available from: https://the socialtalks.com/technology/meta-reworks-its-doxxing-policies-andputs-an-end-to-a-dangerous-loophole/ [Accessed 3 July 2022]

Solanke, I. (2017) *Discrimination as Stigma: A Theory of Anti-Discrimination Law*, London: Bloomsbury Publishing.

Southern Poverty Law Center, The (2011) '10 anti- gay myths debunked', available from: www.splcenter.org/fighting-hate/intelligence-report/2011/10-anti-gay-myths-debunked [Accessed 9 August 2022]

Southern Poverty Law Center, The (2020a) 'Anti- LGBTQ', available from: www.splcenter.org/fighting-hate/extremist-files/ideology/anti-lgbtq [Accessed 14 March 2021]

Southern Poverty Law Center, The (2020b) *The Year in Hate and Extremism*, Montgomery: The Southern Poverty Law Center.

Southerton, C., D. Marshall, P. Aggleton, M.L. Rasmussen and R. Cover (2021) 'Restricted modes: Social media, content classification and LGBTQ sexual citizenship', *New Media & Society*, 23(5): 920–38.

Spangler, T. (2019) 'Sustained attacks on gay Latino journalist', available from: https://variety.com/2019/digital/news/youtube-harassment-policies-attacks-gay-latino-carlos-maza-steven-crowder-1203234645/ [Accessed 8 February 2023]

Spata, C. (2019) 'Drag Queen Story Hour in St. Petersburg draws protesters: We went inside', *Tampa Bay Times*, available from: www.tampabay.com/news/2019/08/14/drag-queen-story-hour-in-st-petersburg-draws-protesters-we-went-inside/ [Accessed 18 March 2021]

Stone, A.L. and J. Cantrell (2015) *Out of the Closet, Into the Archives: Researching Sexual Histories*, Albany: SUNY Press.

Stone, D.R. (2018a) 'Censorship dateline', *Journal of Intellectual Freedom and Privacy*, 3(2–3): 18–40.

Stone, D.R. (2018b) 'From the bench', *Journal of Intellectual Freedom and Privacy*, 3(2–3): 41–69.

Stone, D.R. (2019a) 'From the bench', *Journal of Intellectual Freedom and Privacy*, 4(1): 54–9.

Stone, D.R. (2019b) 'Drag Queen Storytimes', *Journal of Intellectual Freedom and Privacy*, 4(3): 51–3.

Stone, D.R. (2019c) 'Drag Queen Storytimes', *Journal of Intellectual Freedom and Privacy*, 4(2): 65–78.

Strand, C. and J. Svensson (2021) *Disinformation Campaigns about LGBTI+ People in the EU and Foreign Influence*, Brussels: European Parliament.

Street, M. (2022) '1st LGBTQ+ cryptocurrency, Maricoin, launches with questionable name', *Advocate*, available from: www.advocate.com/business/2022/1/03/1st-lgbtq-cryptocurrency-maricoin-launches-questionable-name [Accessed 6 July 2022]

Sullivan, W.F. (2018) *The Impossibility of Religious Freedom: New Edition*, Princeton, NJ: Princeton University Press.

Swenson, A. (2022) 'Posts falsely claim drag performer exposed self to children', *AP News*, available from: https://apnews.com/article/fact-check-drag-queen-story-hour-photo-965766299271 [Accessed 24 June 2022]

Tatum, M. (2022) 'Meet the LGBTQ activists fighting to be themselves online in Malaysia', *MIT Technology Review*, available from: www.technologyreview.com/2022/06/08/1053212/lgbtq-activists-online-in-malaysia/ [Accessed 6 July 2022]

Taylor, J. (2020) 'Police took three years to make finding against officer who slammed teen to ground at 2013 Sydney Mardi Gras', *The Guardian*, available from: www.theguardian.com/australia-news/2020/jun/04/police-took-three-years-to-dismiss-officer-who-slammed-teen-in-to-ground-at-2013-sydney-mardi-gras [Accessed 28 January 2021]

Thepsourinthone, J., T. Dune, P. Liamputtong and A. Arora (2020) 'The relationship between masculinity and internalized homophobia amongst Australian gay men', *International Journal of Environmental Research and Public Health*, 17(15): 5475.

Thomas, S. (2022) 'Drag event in Melbourne postponed after protests threats from neo-Nazis', Star Observer, available from: www.starobserver.com.au/news/drag-event-in-melbourne-postponed-after-protests-threats-from-neo-nazis/219103 [Accessed 8 December 2022]

Tiffany, K. (2022) 'Doxxing means whatever you want it to', *The Atlantic*, available from: www.theatlantic.com/technology/archive/2022/04/doxxing-meaning-libs-of-tiktok/629643/ [Accessed 2 July 2022]

Tomsen, S. (2002) *Hatred, Murder and Male Honour: Anti-Homosexual Homicides in New South Wales, 1980–2000*, Australian Institute of Criminology Research and Public Policy Series 43, Canberra: Australian Institute of Criminology.

Towle, A. (2020) 'Young Conservative who protested Drag Queen Story hour dies by suicide hours after going viral', *Towleroad*, available from: https://www.towleroad.com/2020/01/wilson-gavin-drag-queen-story-hour/ [Accessed 22 July 2021]

Tran, D., C.T. Sullivan and L. Nicholas (2022) 'Lateral violence and microaggressions in the LGBTQ+ community: A scoping review', *Journal of Homosexuality*, DOI: 10.1080/00918369.2021.2020543.

Tremblay, M.-C. (2020) 'The wicked interplay of hate rhetoric, politics and the internet: What can health promotion do to counter right-wing extremism?', *Health Promotion International*, 35(1): 1–4.

Triggs, A.H., K. Møller and C. Neumayer (2021) 'Context collapse and anonymity among queer Reddit users', *New Media & Society*, 23(1): 5–21.

Trott, V.A. (2020) '"Gillette: The best a beta can get": Networking hegemonic masculinity in the digital sphere', *New Media & Society*, 24(6): 1417–34.

Tyler, I. (2020) *Stigma: The Machinery of Inequality*, London: Bloomsbury Publishing.

United Nations General Assembly (2019) *Surveillance and Human Rights: Report of the Special Rapporteur on the Promotion and Protection of the Right to Freedom of Expression and Opinion*, A/HRC/41/35, available from: www.ohchr.org/en/documents/thematic-reports/ahrc4135-surveillance-and-human-rights-report-special-rapporteur [Accessed 21 November 2022]

US Department of Homeland Security (2020) 'Department of Homeland Security releases homeland threat assessment', available from: www.dhs.gov/news/2020/10/06/department-homeland-security-releases-homeland-threat-assessment [Accessed 27 January 2021]

US Federal Bureau of Investigation (n.d.) 'What we investigate: Hate crimes', available from: www.fbi.gov/investigate/civil-rights/hate-crimes [Accessed 20 May 2021]

Valocchi, S. (2017) 'Capitalisms and gay identities: Towards a capitalist theory of social movements', *Social Problems*, 64(2): 315–31.

Valverde, M. (2010) 'Practices of citizenship and scales of governance', *New Criminal Law Review*, 13(2): 216–40.

Valverde, M. (2015) *Chronotopes of Law: Jurisdiction, Scale and Governance*, Oxford: Routledge.

van der Toorn, J., R. Pliskin and T. Morgenroth (2020) 'Not quite over the rainbow: The unrelenting and insidious nature of heteronormative ideology', *Current Opinion in Behavioral Sciences*, 34: 160–5.

van Nuenen, T., J. Such and M. Cote (2022) 'Intersectional experiences of unfair treatment caused by automated computational systems', *Proceedings of the ACM on Human-Computer Interaction for Computing Machinery*, 6(CSCW2): 1–30.

Verrelli, S., F.A. White, L.J. Harvey and M.R. Pulciani (2019) 'Minority stress, social support, and the mental health of lesbian, gay, and bisexual Australians during the Australian Marriage Law Postal Survey', *Australian Psychologist*, 54(4): 336–46.

REFERENCES

Wakabayashi, D. (2020) 'Legal shield for social media is targeted by Trump', *The New York Times*, available from: www.nytimes.com/2020/05/28/business/section-230-internet-speech.html [Accessed 3 July 2020]

Walker-Munro, B. (2022) 'What do TikTok, Bunnings, eBay and Netflix have in common? They're all hyper-collectors', *The Conversation*, available from: https://theconversation.com/what-do-tiktok-bunnings-ebay-and-netflix-have-in-common-the yre-all-hyper-collectors-187274 [Accessed 21 November 2022]

Wallace-Wells, B. (2019) 'David French, Sohrab Ahmari, and the battle for the future of conservatism', *The New Yorker*, available from: www.newyorker.com/news/the-political-scene/david-fre nch-sohrab-ahmari-and-the-battle-for-the-future-of-conservat ism [Accessed 8 March 2021]

Wang, Y. and M. Kosinski (2018) 'Deep neural networks are more accurate than humans at detecting sexual orientation from facial images', *Journal of Personality and Social Psychology*, 114(2): 246.

Weber, C. (2015) 'Why is there no queer international theory?', *European Journal of International Relations*, 21(1): 27–51.

Weber, P. (2020) 'Queer perspectives on digital research: A conversation with Mary Gray', available from: https://items.ssrc.org/sexual ity-gender-studies-now/queer-perspectives-on-digital-research-a-conversation-with-mary-gray/ [Accessed 22 October 2021]

Weeks, J. (2017) *Sex, Politics and Society: The Regulation of Sexuality Since 1800*, London: Routledge.

Weiss, M.L. (2007) 'We know who you are. We'll employ you': Non-discrimination and Singapore's bohemian dreams', in M.V.L. Badgett and J. Frank (eds) *Sexual Orientation Discrimination: An International Perspective*, New York: Routledge, pp 164–76.

Wiedlitzka, S., G. Prati, R. Brown, J. Smith and M.A. Walters (2021) 'Hate in word and deed: The temporal association between online and offline islamophobia', *Journal of Quantitative Criminology*, 39: 75–96.

Willett, G. (2000) *Living out Loud: A History of Gay and Lesbian Activism in Australia*, Sydney: Allen & Unwin.

Williams, M.L., P. Burnap, A. Javed, H. Liu and S. Ozalp (2020) 'Hate in the machine: Anti-Black and anti-Muslim social media posts as predictors of offline racially and religiously aggravated crime', *The British Journal of Criminology*, 60(1): 93–117.

Williamson, H. (2015) 'Misogyny and homophobia: Patriarchy, gender policing, and the male gaze', *Open Democracy*, available from: www.opendemocracy.net/en/5050/misogyny-and-hom ophobia-patriarchy-gender-policing-and-male-gaze/ [Accessed 11 August 2022]

Wood, M.A. (2021) 'Rethinking how technologies harm', *The British Journal of Criminology*, 61(3): 627–47.

Wotherspoon, G. (2016) *Gay Sydney: A History*, Sydney: New South Publishing.

Wu, X. and X. Zhang (2016) 'Automated inference on criminality using face images', *ArXiv*, abs/1611.04135.

Wuest, J. (2021) 'From pathology to "born perfect": Science, law, and citizenship in American LGBTQ+ advocacy', *Perspectives on Politics*, 19(3): 838–53.

Youde, J. (2019) 'The global HIV/AIDS and LGBT movements', in M.J. Bosia, S.M. McEvoy and M. Rahman (eds) *The Oxford Handbook of Global LGBT and Sexual Diversity Politics*, New York: Oxford University Press, pp 301–14.

Yue, A. and R.P. Lim (2022) 'Digital sexual citizenship and LGBT young people's platform use', *International Communication Gazette*, 84(4): 331–48.

Zedner, L. (2007) 'Pre-crime and post-criminology?', *Theoretical Criminology*, 11(2): 261–81.

Zuboff, S. (2019) *The Age of Surveillance Capitalism: The Fight for a Human Future at the New Frontier of Power*, London: Profile Books.

Index

Printed and bound by CPI Group (UK) Ltd, Croydon, CR0 4YY